I0138575

PREACHING
THAT CONNECTS

Charles B. Bugg AND Alan Redditt

Smyth & Helwys Publishing, Inc.
6316 Peake Road
Macon, Georgia 31210-3960
1-800-747-3016
©2016 by Chuck Bugg and Alan Redditt
All rights reserved.

Library of Congress Cataloging-in-Publication Data

Names: Bugg, Charles B., author.
Title: Preaching that connects / by Charles B. Bugg and Alan Redditt.
Description: Macon : Smyth & Helwys, 2016.
Identifiers: LCCN 2016020184 | ISBN 9781573128872 (pbk. : alk. paper)
Subjects: LCSH: Preaching.
Classification: LCC BV4211.3 .B835 2016 | DDC 251--dc23
LC record available at https://lccn.loc.gov/2016020184

Disclaimer of Liability: With respect to statements of opinion or fact available in this work of nonfiction, Smyth & Helwys Publishing Inc. nor any of its employees, makes any warranty, express or implied, or assumes any legal liability or responsibility for the accuracy or completeness of any information disclosed, or represents that its use would not infringe privately-owned rights.

Dedications

To Megan
—AR

I want to dedicate my part of this book to the three people who have heard me preach the most and still love me. My wife, Diane, has been my "Barnabas" through my ministry. Diane has encouraged me and loved me in a way that has enriched my life more than I can say.

Laura Beth, our older child, followed her dad into the world of theology. Laura Beth received her MDiv and ThD from the Harvard Divinity School and teaches at the University of Toronto in Canada. Not only are Diane and I proud of Laura Beth, but we are also very proud of our son-in-law, Bryan, and our grandson, Finn. When you have lots of time, I'll tell you about the best and brightest grandchild in the world.

Our son, David, has shown us grace and courage through his own suffering. Diagnosed when he was ten with a malignant brain tumor, David has walked through the Valley of the Shadow of Death and has emerged as the kindest, most sensitive, and most caring person I know.

Thanks seems like too small a word, but from my depths, thanks to the three of you for all that you have meant and continue to mean to me.

—CB

Acknowledgments

We wish to thank Mrs. Devin Harris-Davis, pastoral resident of Georgetown Baptist Church, for transcribing the conversation that became chapter 8.

And in honor of the connection God brought about with the congregations of

Worthington

Faith

Frankfort

Covington

Conway

St. Charles Avenue

Georgetown

—AR

No preacher is complete without people who give him the gift of listening. I want to say how much it has meant to be your pastor, your interim pastor, or even your preacher for a day.

No professor is complete without students who give him the gift of listening. Thanks to you for letting me be part of your lives for a season. I'm proud of each of you, even the ones who took the required course kicking and screaming.

Finally, I want to thank Keith Gammons and the excellent team at Smyth & Helwys. You have honored me by allowing me to publish under your banner.

—CB

Contents

Introduction

Charles Bugg

When I had the idea for this book, I thought about how stimulating it would be for me to share the task of writing it with a minister I respect. The town of Georgetown, Kentucky, where our family now lives, has several outstanding preachers. Any one of them would have added rich flavor to this book.

Out of this group of possibilities, Alan Redditt kept emerging. He is not only half my age, which gives a different generational perspective, but he is also an exceptional preacher. In the times I've heard him preach, I have been impressed by his insights, his superb use of biblical texts, and his delivery that is both natural and commands listeners' attention.

Alan is pastor of the Georgetown Baptist Church in Georgetown, Kentucky. He was raised in Georgetown, graduated from Georgetown College, and has earned graduate degrees from McAfee Divinity School and the Divinity School at Duke University.

On the other hand, my family and I came to Kentucky to retire. After all my wanderings as a pastor and seminary professor, I promised Diane we would retire in her home state. We marry for better or for worse. Right now, it's February as I'm writing, snow and ice blanket the ground, and it's bitterly cold. I was raised in Florida, where I never saw snow for the first twenty-two years of my life. My wife and I could be playing shuffleboard in some sunny retirement village in the Sunshine State, but I made a promise. Kentucky it is, and I wait for the spring to come.

Fortunately, retirement hasn't meant staying home and sitting in a recliner. I teach adjunctively at Georgetown College and at the Baptist Seminary of Kentucky. In addition, I have been interim pastor of several churches, but I've told Diane to let me know when my sermons either make no sense or I fall into sentimental reminiscing. Up to this point in my life, I have resisted playing golf as a time-consuming hobby. However, I may have to change, buy some clubs and balls, and be prepared to yell "fore" at anybody in range of my errant shot.

That's enough about my future. What are Alan and I trying to accomplish in this book? Most people might think writing about preaching to connect deals with a minister's presentation that connects to her hearers. Do we hear what she says? Do we understand what she says, or is she giving us an upper-level divinity school class in theology, complete with esoteric terms and strange-sounding theological words? Maybe, most importantly, do we sense that the minister knows what it is to be a human being and cares about us as fellow strugglers?

In chapter 1, I offer a metaphor for preaching. In a profound sense, preaching is the offering of ourselves and our gifts to the God who has made us in God's image. Therefore, preaching is the offering of ourselves to God. We don't need to imitate someone else.

Connecting with the holy is a subject that Alan addresses in chapter 2. Those of us who have been in ministry know how easy it is for our spirits to be captured by the business of the church and by the negative criticism that we sometimes face. I had the privilege of being the pastor of churches of different sizes. Regardless of whether we like to refer to the church as a business, it certainly has the elements of a business. We count money, count people, care for buildings, and have church conferences with reports from committees that basically talk about some aspect of the church and how we are doing.

The constant drumbeat of the church as a business can take a serious toll on the spiritual lives of ministers. First, few of us have been trained to be a chief executive officer. Most of the classes we took to prepare us for ministry taught us to think theologically, exegete a biblical text, prepare a sermon, care for the needs of people, and be, as Dr. Wayne Oates titled one of his books, *The Christian Pastor.*

Second, and perhaps even more significant, most of us entered ministry with the idea that we were called to model the Christian faith for our parishioners. We assumed that an intimate relationship with God came with our ordination certificates. We knew we were far from perfect, but we thought we would preach love, faith, and hope and show through our lives how those things gave us a sense of balance and care for ourselves and other people. The thud you just heard is the Reverend Humpty Dumpty falling off the wall.

We get caught up in our fears and frustrations. We become sad that we walk by on the other side of the deepest needs of our spouses and children. That sadness may manifest itself in anger, and we live with a seething rage toward ourselves and anyone who may have a helpful word of negative criticism for us.

Of course, the ultimate sadness is that we lose any sense of God's presence. We become distracted or allow ourselves to get sloppy in our spiritual disciplines. Spirituality assumes intentionality, and the fact is that even ministers—maybe ministers most of all—need to be intentional in the care of our own souls.

Fortunately, Alan is a product of some of our newer divinity schools, which are putting a priority on the spiritual formation of the clergy. At the same time, Alan has been pastor long enough to know that what sounded obvious in the classroom can be obscured in the demands of the congregation. Suddenly, the pastor loses himself in the clutter of committee meetings, conflicts, and complex expectations from church members.

How does the minister stay focused on the holy when the daily demands of the church seem relentless? How do we come to the preaching event with a sense that God is working in us and through us? Or do we just "get up" sermons similar to the way we're trying to "get up" enough energy to do whatever we have to do in our ministries?

What about connecting with ourselves? I will write about this in chapter 3, because most of my life I have tried to imitate some well-known preacher and have lost my authenticity in the process. Theologically, it's an issue of grace. Do we believe that God has made us worthy enough, or do we have to assume a different voice and "persona" when we enter the pulpit?

People can spot a phony even when she stands behind the pulpit. In my opinion, the day is over for "pulpit giants" or for ministers who have the same vocal inflections and pulpit choreography as five other preachers in town. Where is the real deal?

Underlying the dissonance between our public and private selves is a lack of love for who God has created us to be. If I believe that God made a mistake in creating me, I will try to get love from others by intimidating someone else or becoming someone hardly recognizable. Often this syndrome is seen in the clergyperson who assumes a "preacher's voice" while proclaiming and who pitches his voice at a level that sounds contrived and unnatural. Can we love ourselves enough to give the gift of our true selves when we preach?

An effective preacher also connects with the biblical text and the biblical word. In chapter 4, I will attempt to portray the preacher as a hybrid of theologian, pastor, and prophet.

In the introduction to chapter 4, I am most concerned with the role of the preacher as theologian. Ultimately, our task is to try to bring the word of God to the burdens that we bear and a challenge for the church to be on mission for God in a broken world.

Not every sermon will comfort and challenge, but all sermons should seek to bring a word from God. This means a pastor is a theologian, looking at life and trying to discern how God is at work and where God's love needs to be shared. Such a calling puts a weight on the pastor. We can't think of theologians as simply professors in the academy who have more time to read and write. Pastors know their congregations, and that is essential to theology. Each Sunday, the minister preaches in a context he knows. That's "localized theology." What better image than a pastor carefully exegeting the text each week, crafting her sermon to speak to people she knows, then preaching a word from God that meets people where they are?

The communication of a message from one person to another is difficult at best, and it doesn't help that we have few structures for dialogue. In most places, preaching is still a monologue, and if the congregation doesn't understand, tough for them. Connecting with our hearers is absolutely important to effective proclamation, and Alan bring his gifts to this chapter (ch. 5). As a younger minister, Alan is connecting with a broad cross-section of people, including a sizable number of students from Georgetown College.

While Alan and I wish that we could give you ten steps to great communication, the fact is that connecting with listeners is a tricky business. The preacher has to be careful not to assume too much. Some of the words we use and some of the assumptions we make about the congregation's biblical knowledge can sabotage the clarity of our message. Unless you are in a highly sophisticated church, I suggest you not use words like "pericope" or begin a sentence like this: "As Rudolf Bultmann says . . . ." Besides, Bultmann is too dated, and a glance at his work shows where we have become stuck in our theological journeys.

From the listener's side, all kinds of things are going on of which ministers are not even aware. People listen in different ways. Some want three clear points, while others delight in a pastor who is like an artist painting a picture, making us all wait until the end to see what it is—or even letting us finish the picture ourselves.

The fact is that our preaching is not writing on the blank slates of our listeners' minds and hearts. Too much is happening in the lives of people for us as ministers to assume that they are processing our words precisely as we speak them. If the listeners are attentive, they are co-creating the sermon with us, and what emerges is not a thoroughbred with sleek lines but a camel with humps. As a preacher, don't be concerned if somebody comes out the back door talking about a hump that wasn't the primary thing you intended him to see and hear.

In chapter 6, Alan will write about connecting with our delivery. In a previous book, I opted for the word *release* instead of *delivery*. Sermons need to be written so they can be internalized in the life of the preacher. Regardless of how we prepare our message, we need to give sufficient time to visualize the movement of the sermon so we are not tethered to our notes or manuscripts when we deliver our sermon.

The reason I chose *release* is that I compared it to the pizza delivery person who brings something to your house but has had no part in making it. No sooner than my book was released than a woman who had delivered several children assured me that *delivery* could have another meaning. I apologize for my obvious oversight and for my sexist blunder.

Despite that apology, I still like the word *release*. To me, it implies eye contact and interaction with the congregation. For all of us who have written our share of papers in school, we have to remember that preaching is oral, and it demands tighter, less complicated sentence structures. Doing this kind of internalizing means that we have to finish our preparation of the written material early enough so that we have time not to memorize it but to internalize the message.

The last chapter of the book, chapter 7, focuses on the important question, "Is there a future for preaching?" Some people are questioning the fundamental concept of proclamation as an oral/aural, mouth-to-ear event. Has it become too boring as a form of communication, particularly in a world where people are used to communicating in multi-sensory ways?

I take the lead in writing this chapter with ample input from Alan. I am particularly interested in his observations about ways to do preaching. While I am not ready to abandon the power of words, I do want to be open to proclamation that uses optic and other sensory devices. Those of us who have preached a long time need to be open-minded to what younger ministers are doing and then decide whether these methods are viable for us in our preaching.

One final word about how Alan and I will approach this book: as we write our chapters, we will share them with each other and then have dialogue about the contents. We have agreed to agree and to disagree, so you may find one of us taking issue with what the other person has said. This is the nature of preaching, isn't it? Put two preachers in a room, and you get not only their opinions but also the opinions of the homileticians who have shaped them.

As preachers, we all yearn and pray to speak words that connect. Alan's and my prayer is that this offering will help in the great calling that God has given us.

Chapter 1

Proclamation as Offering

Before the various connections of preaching are discussed, can we settle on a metaphor that guides our theology of proclamation? Phillips Brooks, famed minister in Boston, stated that his vision of preaching was "truth through personality." His metaphorical statement captured the imaginations of generations of ministers.

When I attended seminary in the 1960s and '70s, this was the underlying aim of every sermon we prepared and preached. The content needed to be truth. While truth means different things to different people, the statement suggested that the substance of a sermon needed to be consistent with an interpretation of the Bible, a theological framework, and with our understanding of the challenges individuals faced and perplexing social problems such as injustice, greed, prejudice, and countless others.

My interpretation of Phillips Brooks is that I try to find the truth and filter that truth through myself, being faithful to my uniqueness as a minister.

While Brooks's metaphor of the preaching event is of great value, I want to skip to our generation and take issue with the image of the preacher as "witness." Largely through the superb writing of

Thomas Long's *The Witness of Preaching*[1] and Anna Carter Florence's *Preaching as Testimony*,[2] the metaphor of witness has become popular for trying to define what ministers do when they preach.

In his memorable example, Long says that the preacher is called to stand behind the pulpit and "tell the truth, the whole truth, and nothing but the truth." Thus, the minister is a witness to eternal truths that he has experienced for himself.

Long and Carter Florence have captured a strong dimension of preaching. What a powerful image to envision a preacher's figuratively raising his right hand and saying to the congregation, "I know this to be true because I have experienced it in my life."

But what about dimensions of faith that we haven't experienced? Do we preach those truths if we have never been a personal witness to them?

Certainly, Tom Long and Anna Carter Florence—as well as other homileticians who use "witness" or "testimony" as metaphors for their proclamation—are astute enough not to restrict preaching to what is personal and can be played out on the small screens of our experiences. Yet someone who is as respected as Tom Long titles his book *The Witness of Preaching*, and the thing some of us hear is that the truth we preach has to be what we've witnessed and experienced.

Do we preach those truths if we have never been a personal witness to them?

While I'm content to retain "witness" as a powerful metaphor for preaching, I believe that other terms need to be added to complete a holistic view of proclamation. What about the preacher as a person giving an offering? Sometimes the offering is within our means. But other times, the biblical and theological truths we point to *are* expressions of our lives but might not be things we have experienced ourselves.

Preaching as Offering

Can we as preachers tell the truth even if that truth is not from our own experience? Or do we have to be a witness to everything we preach? The word "offering" may seem like a strange metaphor for preaching. In most of our church services, the offertory is the time when we give money to the work of God through the church. In fact, pastors who have to sweat out budget requirements versus deficiencies in a church's giving will probably say that many parishioners are not giving up to their means, much less sacrificially beyond their means.

Ministers resort to all kinds of euphemisms when they preach about the offering. The word "money" is so seldom heard as the minister walks around the walls of Jericho blowing a trumpet that if the song had lyrics, they would probably be "give all your talent, time, and love."

Preaching Beyond Our Means

The word "offering" seems to be an apt metaphor for proclamation. First, we are called to preach beyond our means. Sometimes a sermon is not going to the witness stand to give testimony about what I have done or seen. Rather, preaching may be standing at the edge of some biblical truth and sharing in a confessional way, "I want us to journey to a place that has the possibility to change all of our lives."

In a class I teach at Georgetown College, I assign projects to students. One of the requirements is that the projects have personal meaning to the students. Some of the students focus on a family crisis, and they seek to find how God may be at work in the midst of their difficulties. One student asked me about a particular problem in his family system. As he struggled to find a biblical text that might shed light on what he faced, I suggested Romans 8:28: "In all things, God works for good to those who love

God and live according to God's purpose." While these words from the Epistle to the Romans are comforting, I told the student that I had never fully experienced the power of this promise in my life.

For example, what does it mean to love God and live according to God's purpose? How do we see that God is putting together the broken pieces of our lives in such a way that it is for our own good? Try telling that to a parent whose child is addicted to heroin or to a widow who has lost her spouse.

Rather, preaching may be standing at the edge of some biblical truth and sharing in a confessional way, "I want us to journey to a place that has the possibility to change all of our lives."

Yet, this promise is in the Bible, and unless we preach only the passages of Scripture to which we can give strong witness and testimony, we now have a truth that is beyond our means. I am making an offering that is more than I possess, but isn't that part of the preacher's calling? Sometimes I have to be honest with listeners that there are things in the Bible to which I wish I could be an unblinking witness, but I am a fellow struggler offering more than I possess.

Second, an offering is designed to be placed in the hands of God and used for God's purposes. Really, what we do is place our gifts in the hands of the church or some charitable institution to be distributed according to the group's budget plans. To think biblically and theologically, what we are doing is placing the gifts of our words in God's hands and trusting the Spirit of God to multiply and empower those offerings.

For those of us who preach, this image has particular resonance. While developing a sermon requires our best efforts, preachers become anxious because they believe the success of the sermon depends solely on their work. Few, if any, preachers are capable of producing a masterpiece each time we come to the pulpit.

When I did a sabbatical study with Fred Craddock, I asked him, "What is the last thing you say to yourself before you enter the pulpit to preach?" I was waiting for the memorable word, the life-altering phrase, or a passage of Scripture that could turn a whimper of a sermon into a thunderbolt. What Craddock said seemed to me, at the time, to be ordinary for such an extraordinary preacher. "The last thing I say to myself before I get up to preach," Craddock said, "is thank you, God, that what happens in the sermon doesn't depend on how I feel about it."

It took me a while to mull over Craddock's response. After some thought, it made great sense. Many ministers are probably like me. To use a baseball analogy, I have gone to the pulpit wanting to hit the ball out of the park. A home run was my goal. The fact is, I have swung and missed more times than I care to admit. On other occasions, if the sermon's been a hit, it's been a "bloop" single to center field, and I was fortunate enough to reach first base.

Craddock's wise words were a reminder for all of us who preach that we do our best to prepare and preach a message, but we begin to play God when we decide—based on our feelings—whether the sermon connected with the listeners. As Craddock would remind us, something more complex and transcendent takes place in the preaching event, and the preacher's feelings are not the ultimate factor in whether the good news is spoken and heard.

Offering and Contemplation

For most who preach, the culmination of our preparation and prayer is an action. For example, we talk about "getting up to preach." Despite the fact that the Bible depicts Jesus sitting down to teach and proclaim, across the years preachers have been the ones to stand while the hearers sit. This made the delivery of the sermon even more important.

Today, the "release" of the message is done in a variety of forms and with various levels of intensity. Some ministers stand behind the pulpit, tethered to their notes or manuscripts; others are peripatetic, wandering in the pulpit area; and some walk up and down the aisles of the church building, awakening those who thought they were going to get a nice nap before lunch.

By its nature, proclamation has two significant shifts. Preparation is the time when the preacher is alone with God, with her thoughts, with the biblical text, with the commentaries, and with images of the parishioners and their needs. Out of that mix come the contours of the sermon.

Then the preacher emerges from the private time to go public. He stands at the house of worship trying to convey the message fashioned in the room of preparation. But what if we could collapse the distance between the private and the public and see the release of the sermon as an act of contemplative offering?

> But what if we could collapse the distance between the private and the public and see the release of the sermon as an act of contemplative offering?

For many, Father Richard Rohr has been a guide in matters of the spirit. Founder and director for the Center for Action and Contemplation in New Mexico, this Roman Catholic priest writes about the affairs of the heart with unusual insight. In *Silent Compassion: Finding God in Contemplation*, Rohr speaks about the close connection between contemplation and compassion. One of his chapters is titled "Looking Out in Prayer with Contemplative Eyes."[3]

While not addressing preaching directly, Rohr discusses the way in which we view people and how contemplation becomes a key avenue to compassion. Those who preach ask ourselves, "How do we see the hearers of our messages? Are they waiting to be won over by our presence and presentation? Are they really not interested in what we have to say, and therefore we feel the need to do something dramatic or unusual to get their attention?"

What we should ask is, "Does the contemplation that filled the room of preparation now fill the room of presentation so that we look at our parishioners with compassion and care?"

> Does the contemplation that filled the room of preparation now fill the room of presentation so that we look at our parishioners with compassion and care?

In this way, the sermon becomes our offering to people we love. We are not out to impress or to see the congregants as against us or even fundamentally different from us. What people need is what the preacher needs. We all need to know the compassion of the Holy One. We are offering hearers not just a stream of words. We are not developing a style of delivery to keep reluctant listeners' attention. We are offering compassion, and when the benediction is announced, we hope the people leaving know that the minister has offered the compassion of the God whose other name is love.

Offering and Distance

Fred Craddock wrote that preachers operate between the polarities of intimacy and distance. For example, in preparing for the sermon, the minister engages a biblical text. While the preacher wants to "know" that passage of Scripture, he never wants to seem as if he owns or possesses it. Good preachers allow the text to live and the hearers to feel its warmth or fire, but at the same time the Bible is not a book to be captured, domesticated, and presented as if it has become a pin on our own chain. The text of Scripture is always more than we can understand and put into words. Thus, in his study the minister struggles to balance intimacy with what Karl Barth called "the strange new world of the Bible."

Preachers also try to achieve balance in the release of the sermon. How do we communicate authenticity and care to our listeners without doing what Michael Brothers calls "crowding" those same hearers?[4] Some of us who preach are so eager for people to respond to our words that our preaching moves from invitation to imposition. We violate the psychic space between ourselves and our hearers. This can be done by a delivery style that is too "in your face" or uses words that *demand* rather than *offer an invitation.*

Seeing preaching as an act of offering may help proclaimers to preserve balance between intimacy and distance. For example, when I give a monetary offering to the church, I want to feel close to it. I hope what I give represents some sacrifice on my part and is a result of the investment of work on my part. At the same time, I don't want to "track" every dime of my offering and make sure it's spent in precisely the way I want.

My offering is a gift. I give it and allow it to flow through the channels of the church and do the work of missions near and far—and also to help pay the salary of my pastor and turn the heat on in the church building during winter. As in the offering of the sermon, I have both attachment to and detachment from what I give. The attachment of a minister to her sermon is normal. She has prayed, studied, and invested much of her mind and heart as she has sought God's leadership in the process. The preacher has expended both physical and spiritual energy as she has delivered her message.

However, the minister must guard against the kind of attachment that says, "This is my message, and you are going to receive it whether you want to or not." This kind of over-attachment results in imposing word choices and a delivery that is overly assertive. The "self-awareness" of the preacher is vitally important. Can I offer this sermon as a gift from God, or will I cross the boundary where the message is so much mine that I can't allow listeners the freedom to respond as God leads?

At the same time, preachers shouldn't become so detached from the importance of what we say that the people who hear us feel that we don't care. It's always a balancing act between attachment and detachment, intimacy and distance, so that the passion of the minister is felt while the integrity and freedom of the hearers are respected.

Notes

1. Thomas Long, *The Witness of Preaching*, 2nd ed. (Louisville KY: Westminster John Knox Press, 2005).

2. Anna Carter Florence, *Preaching as Testimony* (Louisville KY: Westminster John Knox Press, 2007).

3. Richard Rohr, *Silent Compassion: Finding God in Contemplation* (Cincinnati: Franciscan Media, 2014).

4. Michael Brothers, *Distance in Preaching: Room to Speak, Room to Listen* (Grand Rapids MI: William B. Eerdmans Publishing Company, 2014) 2.

Chapter 2

Connecting with the Holy

Preaching ministry joins at least three conversations or relationships already in progress. These three conversations, between Holy and creation, Holy and church, and Holy and pastor, began long before the arrival of a pastor in any preaching event and continue long after the sermon delivery has concluded. Sometimes distinct from one another, but often overlapping, these conversations help the minister remain in tune with the dance between the underlying mysteries of divine inspiration and humility about the human filter.

Conversation between Holy and Creation

In his wonderful book exploring family systems theory from an evangelical perspective, Peter Scazzero describes the limit God established in the life of King David by refusing to allow David to construct the temple. Scazzero interprets this passage, writing, "David accepted that his breadth of knowledge was too narrow to perceive God's intent. Only time would strip away his shallow understandings of what was going on and why God said 'no' to his plans. God was painting on a vast canvas over a long period of time. Only in eternity would he understand."[1] This summary aptly describes the mysterious relationship between God and cosmos, Creator and creature, into which the preacher steps.

The original setting for conversation between Holy and creation occurs in the forms of *Sabbath* and *prayer*. The creation accounts of Genesis 1 and 2 include the basis for these spiritual disciplines. At the end of the seven-day creation account of Genesis 1, God rests. Subsequent aspects of Sabbath build on this foundation, including worship and play/leisure. In the midst of the garden creation account that follows in Genesis 2 and 3, conversation occurs between Creator and creature, thus providing the basis for all types of prayer that follow.

While it may seem intimidating to consider the dialogue between Creator and creation, doing so encourages me to stay aware of the larger metanarratives in Holy Scripture. One of the most rewarding spiritual practices for me as a preaching minister is to recognize where an individual passage of Scripture and my limited insight into it connect with one of the overarching themes of the Hebrew Bible and New Testament. Such connections give me a sense of shared journey with earlier ministers and believers, who wrestled with the same issues and celebrated the same grace and mercy as I.

Unfortunately, such connections concerning Scripture specifically and life generally often elude me! A spiritual discipline that has shaped my life perhaps more than any other in the last several years has been a serious commitment to *pastoral peer relationships*. I do all I can to maintain four such groups:

• A *local peer group* from across central and eastern Kentucky, consisting of mentors, friends, and colleagues who span several generations. We mostly talk life, albeit the life of a minister. We meet monthly, and though none of us makes it to every session, we never miss as a group. This is survival stuff.

• A *mentoring group* with the pastor of one of the leading churches in our region. Six or eight ministers in our first time serving as permanent senior pastors meet with our mentor pastor approximately five times annually. We mostly talk shop, with the understanding that though it appears we are discussing questions about how to handle different aspects of church leadership and the balance with family life, a tremendous struggle lies below the surface. Many times the conversation with eight ministers draws to a close, but the person-to-person support continues through discussion in the hallway or parking lot.

• A *regional peer group* across state lines. We meet once a year for a few days of retreat, which includes meals, ballgames, and serious reflection on agreed-upon topics. This is conference- and seminar-quality insight and feedback coupled with a time allotment that allows new friendships to develop in a restful, reflective context.

• A *local ministerial association* with participation across ecumenical lines. Breakfast gatherings at the local diner yield warm fellowship punctuated by belly laughs and tearful confession, but it is also in these settings that we plan annual events like the Community Thanksgiving Meal and Good Friday noontime service. While important theological differences remain, we find many ways to affirm that we are all in this together.

Conversation between Holy and Church

On a smaller scale (yet remarkably mysterious in its own right), the discussion between God and the local church plays out over generations. This conversation constitutes something bigger than the Lectionary or expository style or topical awareness. It's bigger than my understanding of the general direction of the church and bigger even than a long-range plan or sense of vision. The church universal joins in the Divine Mission to love the world into relationship through Jesus Christ.

Though there is mystery, there is also direction. For example, pastors occasionally encounter the parishioner who says, "I will never forget the sermon when you preached on x," a topic I know full well I have never broached. Nevertheless, something beyond me, something Holy, happened in that person's life during the sermon event.

The Apostle Paul and other New Testament authors sometimes referenced the athletic arena to describe the Christian life (e.g., 1 Cor 9:24-27; Gal 2:2, 5:7; Phil 2:16, 3:14; 1 Tim 4:7; Heb 12:1). In a similar sense, one helpful description of the pastoral role is that a preaching pastor (indeed, any minister) carries a baton much like a runner who runs one leg of a relay race. The individual runner may carry unique roles depending on the circumstances in each portion of the race (lead leg, running the curve, anchor leg), but she has only partial responsibility for the overall outcome of the event. At some point she will receive and/or hand off the baton to other runners. In a similar way, the preacher steps into a role that was previously filled by others and will eventually cede the privilege to successors.

The late twentieth and early twenty-first centuries have brought an unprecedented complexity to this conversation. In any week, many worshipers gather for community worship having already viewed a sermon on screen or listened via podcast. Perhaps an even higher percentage of disciples will gather for Bible study having read church-related literature written and/or published by a different Christian tradition. Like so much else in life, this reality may present good, bad, ugly, or other consequences depending on the situation, but it highlights one simple principle. Local church pastors increasingly have one tool at their disposal: personal relationships with the church. (In chapter 5, "Connecting with Our Listeners," we will explore the importance of pastoral relationship further.)

In many ways, our predecessors in the church lay a foundation for our preaching ministry. In the Baptist church, a predecessor may have introduced the congregation to the seasons of Advent or Lent. In certain settings, a strong sense of local tradition in worship may precede the arrival of the new preacher. Examples might include a special form of lay-led prayer or a particular expectation from the congregation for themed services at several occasions throughout the year. In many instances, a wise pastor recognizes these milestones as markers of the relationship between Holy and church and learns to adapt personal preferences graciously. In other words, the pastor humbly joins a conversation already in progress and attempts to support the health already present, since it originates primarily from what the Holy One has been doing for some time.

Conversation between Holy and Pastor

The conversation between Holy and Pastor exists in at least three overlapping ways: an ongoing conversation, a conversation during sermon preparation, and a conversation at the time of sermon delivery. Perhaps the most obvious aspect of connecting with the Holy is the conversation between the Holy and the pastor. When pastors encourage their congregations with the phrase "remember your baptism," they speak those words to themselves as well. Each of us remains a work in progress, with the Spirit of the Living God continuing to make us new creations in Christ. A parallel phrase that might suit the unique role of the minister would be "remember your calling" or other similar moments of affirmation and seasons of discernment, such as ordination or ecclesial endorsement for chaplains.

This *ongoing conversation* begins in the earliest stages of awareness of the Holy, matures with a personal decision to follow Christ, and finds fruition as a pastor accepts the call to gospel ministry. This conversation continues regardless of and in addition to the pastoral identity of the preacher. In other words, the preacher connects with the Holy in ways other than preaching, and the preacher also happens to connect with the Holy through preaching. Furthermore, the preacher connects with the Holy before arriving at the preaching event or even the preparation of the sermon. Indeed, beneath all the roles and responsibilities of the proclaimer, the individual stands before the Holy, hopefully within the context of nurturing faith community. Thus, the conversation that occurs between preacher and Holy at the time of preparation and delivery is merely an extension of the dialogue that has already long been happening.

For the dual and often-intertwined purposes of personal spiritual health and preaching, pastors will need strong spiritual disciplines.[2] In the last few years, the practice of regular retreats has become one of the most helpful spiritual disciplines for me. When I first attempted to observe retreat days, I found myself allowing many other tasks to crowd out what was originally supposed to be a full day. In saying yes to various thirty-minute or one-hour projects, I carved up my retreat day into something that did not at all resemble what I set out to accomplish. A peaceful, uninterrupted, large block of time is needed. Eventually, rather informally and quite in hindsight, I finally developed best practices for myself. To have a successful retreat, there are several things I need to do:

1. Schedule early. I will sometimes schedule a year's worth of quarterly retreat days (generally two each for spiritual retreat and sermon retreat) at a time.

2. Communicate my schedule and expectations to the team. Several weeks before my event, I share with the church staff that it is on my calendar. We talk about what needs to happen on that day. In particular, our administrative secretary has an excellent understanding of the rare times she will need to contact me while I am away. On the other hand, she knows that I may reach out to her

electronically throughout the day if there is information I need in my sermon planning.

3. Encourage and support others who wish to explore this same discipline. The rest of the team, and especially the other ministers, need to know that I wholeheartedly desire for them to be growing in their spiritual disciplines, too. When I help them identify opportunities for retreat and protect their days when they take them, they provide excellent support to me as well.

On a personal retreat, I will spend a day away from the office primarily in silence and prayer. Over the course of several hours of solitude, I undergo a fairly broad range of experiences. In the early hours, I find myself silencing urges to spend the time on other important tasks. It is helpful to move into these moments with the Jesus Prayer or another similar centering prayer, for I find that the stillness brings vital thoughts to the surface.[3] I may either jot these down or let them go, but when I have captured the thought, I immediately return to the practice of prayer.

Sermon retreats are quite different for me. The setting for such a day is usually a private area of a library or similar space where I can work without interruption from technology or office busyness. I take certain parts of my office with me (study Bible, sermon notebook, tablet device for music, Bible dictionary, calendar) and purposefully leave others behind (computer, monographs, interruptions). Here I pull out all of the sermon ideas that God has provided since my last retreat and start looking for areas of overlap that might be the beginnings of a sermon or topical series. By the end of the day, I typically have several months' worth of sermon texts and/or topics, which I then email to the rest of the worship team.

Mature congregations should not force their ministers to use vacation time for such vital life-giving practices as these retreats or the peer/mentoring groups described above. In particular, any church that has already created a sabbatical policy for its ministers is more than ready to adopt a policy for retreats. For churches without a sabbatical policy, I would recommend that established ministers seek out a conversation with a trusted member of the personnel committee or similar administrative structure. In many settings, lay leaders easily grasp the importance of making retreat time available for ministers. The matter may be resolved as simply as revising an existing policy within a personnel handbook to transition the classic two-week "revival" time into a more flexible option for revivals, retreats, and mission trips. Ideally, lay leaders will even volunteer to champion this cause on behalf of ministers.

Of course, the connection between the Holy and the pastor finds especially meaningful expression *during sermon preparation.* For most ministers, there is significant overlap between devotional life and sermon preparation. What begins as a quick moment of research on a particular topic may lead to an extended period of reflection and prayer on a topic tangential to the sermon for which I am preparing. There are simply moments where the Holy breaks into the scheduled time of sermon preparation with a spiritual insight—or a reflective pause or sense of the nearness of God—that proves to be unrelated to the material at hand.

Out of the abundance of such awareness, the minister offers a sermon. I recently attended a lecture series during which I found myself amazed at the skill of the speaker. She spoke well, with clever turns of phrase, wove scriptural quotations and references throughout her comments with seeming ease, and naturally dropped humor into her remarks. There were moments when I couldn't help reflecting on what an outstanding speaker she was, able to do much that I simply cannot do. It would have been easy for me to shrink back and come away feeling defeated about my inability to speak like the lecturer. In such times, I find it helpful to be reminded that my calling is to a specific ministry context: these people, this place, this time. In other words, my role is to give the best of my gifts, combined with the best of what God has given me. Therefore, I often find myself praying, "What have you given me that I am missing?"

One challenge for new ministers in some traditions is finding enough opportunities to gain experience with preaching. Unfortunately, a candidate's lack of experience with preaching requires a pulpit committee to make a leap of faith in choosing to believe that the candidate has the necessary spiritual disciplines to sustain regular preaching. In the era of civic religion following World War II, many pastors found ample opportunities to preach as young adults or even as teenagers. The erosion of this structure is well documented. What remains of the civic religion era are other institutions that permit and welcome guest preachers, such as nursing homes and other residential facilities, mission centers, prisons and jails, and other settings that value the good news of Christ while lacking resources for full-time clergy coverage. In addition, at least one new organization in the twenty-first century, the Academy of Preachers, now emphasizes the importance of creating preaching opportunities for young people of many different branches of the tree of Christian heritage. Young ministers can gain experience through AoP national, regional, and campus events, as well as AoP breakout sessions at conferences and denominational gatherings.[4]

Finally, the conversation between the Holy and the pastor continues and may even peak *at the time of sermon delivery*. More extemporaneous traditions place a higher degree of importance here, yet for any successful preaching ministry there must be some value on awareness of the Holy despite what has been written or left unwritten during hours of preparation. What minister has not jotted down a last-minute addition to the sermon just before the service begins? Who has not stood to preach only to discover the surprise return of a beloved church member from cancer treatments? Who hasn't had the pieces fit together in new and surprising ways during the sermon? The more I am able to get out of my manuscript and deliver the sermon from a general familiarity with the message, the more I am able to remain open to ongoing conversation with the Holy during delivery.

Many pastors find it helpful to adopt a certain set of practices in the moments leading up to sermon delivery. Such a routine might include reading a sermon or a Scripture passage that reframes the sermon event theologically. Occasionally, a preacher may need to adjust distracting structures or customs in the church, such as asking leaders to hold criticisms until after services have concluded.

One such practice might be to pray with an awareness of these overlapping conversations with the Holy and express a desire to join into them fully through the sermon. The prayer might sound something like this:

> Loving God, thank you for the privilege it is to preach.
>
> Please speak through me, and please speak in spite of me.
>
> Help us to set aside the distractions of the day and focus on nothing but the worship of you, our God.
>
> Please receive the praises of your people and move in such a way that we would be renewed and transformed by your Holy Spirit.
>
> Make us more like Jesus.

I am amazed again and again that the grandness of the Holy can be experienced by little ol' me. The wise minister will build such practices into the living of everyday life and the ongoing rhythms of sermon development. While there may be moments when the Holy breaks surprisingly into my routine, and there may be seasons in which my experience feels more mundane or distant, it is also true that the God we seek to make known through proclamation also desires to be known by proclaimers.

Notes

1. Peter Scazzero, *The Emotionally Healthy Church: A Strategy for Discipleship that Actually Changes Lives* (Grand Rapids: Zondervan, 2003) 151.

2. Examples of helpful resources on spiritual disciplines include Adele Ahlberg Calhoun, *Spiritual Disciplines Handbook: Practices that Transform Us*; Richard J. Foster, *Celebration of Discipline: The Path to Spiritual Growth*; E. Glenn Hinson, *Spiritual Preparation for Christian Leadership*; and Marjorie J. Thompson, *Soul Feast: An Invitation to the Christian Spiritual Life*.

3. I have found the following progression of different breath prayers from Scripture to be quite helpful in bringing stillness to my mind and openness to my heart.

"Speak Lord / your servant is listening." (1 Sam 3:9)

Breathing *in*: Speak Lord

Breathing *out*: Your servant is listening.

Other possibilities include "Be still and know / that I am God" (Psalm 46:10); "Create in me / a clean heart, O God / and renew a right spirit / within me" (Psalm 51:10); The Jesus Prayer: "Lord, Jesus Christ / Son of God / Have mercy on me / A Sinner."

4. Learn more at http://www.academyofpreachers.net/.

Chapter 3

Connecting with Ourselves

What does it mean to connect with ourselves? In preaching, there is sometimes a tendency to be uncomfortable with who we are. Maybe we don't like the pitch of our voices. Perhaps we know a minister who does preaching a certain way, and he seems to be successful. We want to preach like him. Therefore, we forget our own gifts and try to emulate this preacher we admire.

Let's face it: there is a temptation not just to learn from those who preach well but to become carbon copies of them. In this process, we lose ourselves, and most

> When we try too hard to be exactly like another preacher, we lose ourselves, and our hearers lose the opportunity to hear the unique person that we are.

of all, our hearers lose the opportunity to hear the unique person that we are.

Theology of Grace and Call

Being ourselves in the pulpit is not just a nice thing to do; it's rooted in a theology of grace and call. Grace is God's unconditional love. It is God's way of saying that at our core we are good, and God loves what God has created. As Frederick Buechner so beautifully says it,

> The Grace of God means something like this: Here is your life—You might never have been, but you are because the party wouldn't have been complete without you. Here is the world. Beautiful and terrible things will happen. Don't be afraid, I am with you. Nothing can ever separate us. It's for you I created the universe. I love you.[1]

Again, grace doesn't mean that we don't learn from others; it means we don't seek to *become* the others. Preachers move into the pulpit knowing that they will be positively and negatively encountered by listeners. If the minister doesn't become defensive, she will learn and grow from some of the criticism. She must come to the pulpit knowing that God loves her and there is no reason to fear.

Frequently, ministers speak of being "called" by God to ministry. While some ministers may speak of a dramatic call, others talk more about an "impression" that they experienced or a recognition that who they were as people matched the expectations of a particular form of ministry. Frequently, the church, as a community of faith, encouraged someone to consider that God may be calling them to a vocational ministry.

As with the grace of God, the theology of the "call" plays a continuing role in keeping people harnessed to the vocations they are pursuing. The idea of call to service is not limited to clergy;

the church affirms that *every* follower of Christ is called to service. However, churches have used the word "call" especially to apply to those who pursue some type of vocational ministry.

Recognizing that some ministers are called to preach as a part of their vocational expression keeps them connected to the Holy One since it is God who calls, and people respond.

Recognizing that some ministers are called to preach as a part of their vocational expression keeps them connected to the Holy One since it is God who calls, and people respond.

God calls us as we are, and while we grow and hopefully improve our skill sets as proclaimers, we are the ones God calls. Therefore, we don't have to be like someone else; the fundamental transaction of the call is between who God is and who the person is.

Coming to Know Ourselves

In ancient Greek philosophy, people were encouraged to know themselves. The same is true of ministers. The sooner we come to know our strengths, our areas for growth, the particular problems that cause us undue stress, and the issues that may lead us to overreact emotionally, the better we will be as ministers.

For those who preach, it's also important to be mindful of the "seasons" of our lives. As young preachers, we may be eager to prove ourselves and to be overly concerned about how we are viewed. Sometimes, this results in a lack of openness to legitimate negative criticism. No preacher emerges full-blown on this scene as a totally skilled proclaimer. This is the time to evaluate ourselves, to listen to those whose openness we value, and to develop ways in which we prepare and deliver sermons.

Ministers who are in their forties and fifties face particular challenges. By this time, our habits have become ingrained, and we may be reluctant to make changes. At this stage, ministers may feel the weight of having "arrived" as a pastor and are reluctant to do something new and unfamiliar. As preachers, we can develop bad habits or personal idiosyncrasies that impede our ability to hear God's word.

Older ministers may find that they lack the energy and stamina that they once had. This is one reason why it's imperative for a minister to develop a physical exercise regimen. Even with that, an older minister may compensate for lack of energy with wisdom about the Bible and life. That doesn't make elderly ministers experts on everything, but life experiences may give them a greater sensitivity and understanding of the difficult problems people often face.

Since I'm in the elderly stage of ministry, I have to remind myself to continue to study, to read—both theological books as well as books that people in the pews may be reading—and to prepare new sermons that keep me fresh.

Preachers Are Different

One of the challenges of writing about preaching these days is the variety of people who are being called to preach. Preachers coming to the pulpit each week, both men and women, represent a range of ethnicities, experiences, and other personal differences. Assuming that one size fits all preachers is not only ridiculous but also dishonors their variety of gifts and styles.

All sermons should have a biblical text, should address some need or challenge of the people who are listening, and should be enunciated clearly. Beyond these requirements, we are hard-pressed to find many essentials. Even the length of the message is subject to debate. While I might suggest twenty to twenty-five minutes, there are some traditions where that is too much, and some faith groups where that doesn't even qualify as a "real sermon."

One of the most significant changes in many faith traditions over the last several years has been the increasing number of women who are becoming the pastors and preaching ministers of congregations. While some denominations have always been open to women as preachers, mainline denominations are seeing more and more pulpits occupied by women.

> If our goal is to impress the congregation with who we are, we lose sight of the fact that speakers are the messengers, not the message.

We want to avoid making generalizations about the differences in the way people proclaim God's word; there should be no dichotomy between a female preacher and a male preacher. There is no such thing as "the" male voice and "the" female voice. Each person is created differently, influenced by different preachers, educated differently, and thus has his or her unique sound. I am particularly interested in seeing what the next generation of women preachers learns from this current, first generation.

Goal of Preaching: Clarity of Message

After a sermon is preached, do the listeners know what the message is and do they believe that it's vital to their lives? Some sermons die a painful death because they have no real point, and if they have a point, it's not important enough to affect people's lives. These types of messages tend to ramble, bouncing from one thought to another. They lack cohesion, and people have a difficult time listening when the sermon has no controlling focus.

More often perhaps, preachers are guilty of trying to say too many things in a sermon. This is why it's imperative that those of us who preach have a clear point and purpose in mind before we plan the message. We need to know what we want to say and what we want the sermon to do before we start putting the message together and hoping that somehow we'll find clarity as we write.

Making clarity the goal in preaching helps preachers avoid certain temptations. Most preachers like for people to like them, and one temptation is to try to dazzle listeners with our language or rhetorical skills. Good language skills and an understanding of the canons of rhetoric are important for a minister; there's no virtue in bad grammar or crude language in the pulpit. However, if our fundamental desire is to impress people with how good a speaker we are, we miss the primary purpose of preaching, which is to communicate a message. Preachers want effective language, moving stories, and an appeal to the head and heart, but all of these are means to the end of communicating a message. If our goal is to impress the congregation with who we are, we lose sight of the fact that speakers are the messengers, not the message.

It's imperative that we not only construct a message but also allow that message to instruct and construct us as ministers.

Focusing on the clarity of the message also keeps us from being anxious about the response. In many faith traditions, the worship service ends with a hymn of invitation or response. People are invited to come to the front of the sanctuary to profess their faith, join the church, or share publicly any other decisions they have made. They are *invited*. Frequently, this time of response follows the sermon, and often the conclusion is drawn that the number of people who respond is directly related to the efficacy of the message.

Some ministers are more effective in inviting people to respond than others. They conclude the message in a way that ties in with their invitation for people to make decisions. Increasingly, preachers may need to abandon some language in issuing the invitation. For example, in Baptist churches we invite people to join a church by letter or by statement. What does that mean to the person who is not familiar with our terminology? Do they need to bring a letter, or do they need to make a public statement about their faith commitment?

With all of this said, the preacher needs to remember that the sermon is her offering, and she doesn't bear the responsibility for the people response. God changes lives, and in our theology, we affirm that the Spirit of God leads us to the most life-altering decisions.

Strive for Authenticity

When preachers enter the pulpit, they want to be credible and trustworthy. Two problems often sabotage both credibility and authenticity. First, we can stop believing what we're saying and go on autopilot. This is why it's imperative that we not only construct a message but also allow that message to instruct and construct us as ministers.

It's not enough to plan a message without taking the time to allow that message to become part of the fabric of our lives. Preachers are the first listeners to their sermons, and if they don't internalize the message, then listeners will probably not hear it at the deepest parts of their lives. Does that mean ministers have to know all the truths of faith? Absolutely not! Our preaching will be limited if we only share what we know and live.

Sometimes ministers need to stand before the challenging texts of Scripture and confess that they, too, are still struggling to live out both the promises and challenges of the Bible. Some people may expect perfection from their ministers, but most people in the congregation know that their preachers are works in progress. An important factor that reinforces authenticity is when the congregation realizes that ministers don't walk on water. Most people, unless they have unrealistic expectations, will appreciate the preacher who lets them know that he is still on the journey to wholeness.

A second factor that reinforces authenticity is the consistency between a preacher's personal and pulpit presence. Preachers have to be conscious of the dynamics of speaking to a congregation versus talking to an individual. When we are preaching, we have to speak forcefully and loudly enough to be heard. When we are talking to an individual or small group, we adjust our volume and other things such as our gestures to fit the context.

The problem is that when we become so different in our preaching style, people who know us in more intimate settings don't even recognize us.

However, the day has passed for what we used to call "pulpit giants." These preachers often assumed an affected voice quality that "sounded like a preacher." Now, hearers prefer a more conversational tone. They want to listen to a preacher who sounds "real." People want to recognize the voice of the preacher they talk with at the grocery store or sit next to at their children's soccer games.

Continue to Grow in Preaching Skills

Every preacher needs to continue to work on improving her skills as a preacher. Two factors often hinder preachers working to improve their skill sets in the pulpit. One factor is the idea that preaching is strictly a transcendent transaction and that God will communicate the truth regardless of our imperfections.

There is enough truth in that statement to cause some preachers not to work to correct any impediments that they bring to the preaching event. It is true that God changes lives. It is true that God is both the subject and object of our proclamation. It is true that preachers pray for God to inspire the words of the message. But it is also true that we can develop idiosyncrasies in our construction and delivery of the message that keep our words from being heard.

That's why it's important for ministers to listen to their own sermons and ask, "What can I do better to make sure the word from God is heard?" Also helpful is a peer group that will give us feedback or a mentor who will point out places we need to grow.

A second factor that often keeps preachers from seeking feedback is a fear of negative criticism. Sometimes the criticism is unsolicited, and preachers need to be alert to parishioners who are negative about everything in the church, including the way we preach. At the same time, ministers should avoid becoming defensive about criticism that is spoken from a sense of love and care for us. Remember that those of us who preach seldom arrive at perfection, no matter how effective some may be in the pulpit.

Hearing negative feedback about our sermons can be especially difficult because we often see preaching as the heart of our vocation. When somebody criticizes our administrative abilities, it usually doesn't affect us as much as when that person criticizes our preaching abilities. Preaching is where we encounter the most people in any part of our ministry, and those of us who preach tend to be more tender and more easily wounded when the criticism is directed at the heart of our identity.

Again, criticism doesn't mean that we are bad preachers; some criticism will be constructive. We listen to the criticism as objectively as we can, try not to take it personally and let it wound us, and then we decide whether the criticism is valid. If it is, and we make changes in our preaching, then we can see that process as one in which we are growing.

Claiming Our Authority

There may be resistance to the statement that preachers need to claim their authority. First, *authority* is not the same as being *authoritarian.* Being authoritarian denotes a style of preaching that claims to have all the answers to life's questions. In this case, the preacher is the only expert in the room, and the congregation listens passively, accepting everything the preacher says as the final word. An authoritarian preacher brooks no disagreement or no questioning of his interpretation of the Bible and matters of faith.

Authority is different. Perhaps the best biblical example of authority occurs at the conclusion of the Gospel of Matthew's Sermon on the Mount. Matthew says, "Now when Jesus had finished saying these things, the crowds were amazed at his teaching, because he taught as one who had authority and not as their scribes" (Matt 7:28-29, NRSV).

Interestingly, the crowds did not react to the portrait of Jesus as the completion of "Torah" or Jewish law. No comments are recorded about anything Jesus said in the Sermon on the Mount. What impressed them was the way Jesus presented the message.

Jesus spoke with authority and not as the scribes. Authority means "freshness." The scribes would cite other scribes and rabbis when they taught, but Jesus taught in a way that showed the message was his, and it was coming through him as a fresh word. Speaking with authority is not being bombastic and preaching as if the minister knows it all. Rather, it is allowing the message to become internalized in the proclaimer, and then the preacher speaks a fresh word that rises from her depths.

Congregations wants ministers to claim that authority. Those who preach are given the great gift of people's attention. Preachers have the ears of their congregations for a span of time, and the tragedy is when we preachers don't use the time to speak passionately about things that make a difference in all our lives. Sometimes listeners need to be challenged and sometimes they need to be comforted, but they always need to be taken seriously by those who preach.

Notes

1. Frederick Buechner, *Wishful Thinking: A Theological ABC* (New York: Harper and Row Publishers, 1973) 34.

2. Deborah Tannen, *Gender and Discourse* (New York: Oxford University Press, 1994).

Chapter 4

Connecting with the Text

A sermon demands a biblical text. Without the use of a text, a speech may be inspiring, educational, or powerful in its impact on the listeners, but without the foundation of a biblical word, it is not a sermon.

Some people, including some preachers, are leery of the Bible. The Bible has been a source of controversy. Extreme factions have turned their interpretations of the Bible into a personal battleground. Fundamentalists have used words like "infallible" or "inerrant" to defend a literal interpretation of the Bible. The Bible is turned into a book of pseudo-science, and preachers of this stripe use it to advocate a literal reading of the creation story and still support such practices as the paternalism that was part of the biblical worldview. Few if any insights that we have gained across the years since the documents of the Bible were written are factored into the interpretation of Scripture.

On the other hand, there are those who debunk the books in the canon of the Bible as little more than good literature on par with some great novel. For these people, the Bible is the "good book" but not a record of the revelation of God.

In reading and studying the Bible, we want to use the best of critical methodology but always with an eye to trying to find a word from God for ourselves.

As a preacher studies a biblical text, she needs to remember that biblical texts have both a past and a present. The texts were written in particular times and places, and therefore the preacher asks, "What did these words mean?" This keeps the preacher anchored and prevents the imposition of meanings that have no connection to the original import of the biblical words.

In reading and studying the Bible, we want to use the best of critical methodology but always with an eye to trying to find a word for God for ourselves.

At the same time, we don't want to stay frozen in the past. Sermons that dwell on "What did it mean?" may be filled with good information, but they often lack the interesting and inspiring quality when the other question is asked: "What does it mean to us (me) *right now?*" A preacher is reading from ancient documents, but he's speaking to people who live, move, and have their being now. Droning on about the dimensions of the Second Temple in Daniel may find an avid listener who has a penchant for temples, but it will probably not get the attention of the person who has lost her job or the couple whose marriage is ripping apart.

As the preacher connects week after week with a biblical text, it is important that he uses a process that becomes ingrained in his mind. We don't want to have to invent the wheel of preparation each time we come to a new sermon.

Selecting a Text

What are some of the ways we can select a text for a sermon? Obviously, preachers have developed various ways. One that I would *not* suggest is allowing the Bible to fall open, putting your finger on a passage, and viewing that text as the Spirit's leadership. If the Bible falls open to the middle, as it's apt to do, you will be feeding your congregation an abnormal number of lessons from Psalms and Proverbs. This approach also leads to the "instant gratification" syndrome. Preachers who allow their Bibles to fall open and blindly point to some passage are prone to move on quickly to subsequent finger pointing until they find a text whose meaning is apparent. That keeps ministers away from some of the best sermons, which come when we stay with a biblical text and won't let it go until it has yielded a message.

The following are some methods for choosing a text that will help ministers avoid the pitfalls of redundancy and instant gratification.

Lectionary

The lectionary is a cluster of texts for various genres in the biblical canon. While there are different lectionaries, the one most used in Protestant circles is the Revised Common Lectionary. Developed by a committee, this lectionary actually has Scripture readings for each day of the week. Naturally, a preacher is most interested in the texts for Sundays.

Four different readings are given. One is from the Hebrew Bible, a second from the Psalter, a third from the Gospels, and a fourth usually from the epistolary section of the New Testament.

The lectionary is divided into a three-year rotation. Year A features the Gospel of Matthew; Year B the Gospel of Mark; and Year C the Gospel of Luke. Readings from the Gospel of John are interspersed throughout the year, but the Synoptic Gospels are given preference.

Ministers who use the lectionary may try to find a common theme in the four texts and preach on that theme. However, the majority of preachers will select one of the texts and use that as the focal point of the message.

Why use the lectionary? What are the advantages for a preacher? First, the biblical texts are already chosen, and the minister doesn't have to spend time trying to find a text. The only decision may be which of the texts will be the focus of the sermon.

Second, the lectionary recognizes the movement of the Christian calendar. The Christian year begins with Advent and moves through the significant moments of the biblical record. Unlike some churches that simply celebrate Christmas and Easter, the lectionary highlights Epiphany, Lent, Pentecost, and numerous other special Sundays. A worshiper at a church where the lectionary is used will have an opportunity to experience the fullness of the Christian year as well as the encouragement to prepare spiritually for crucial times such as Christmas and Easter.

Third, observance of the lectionary connects churches across denominational lines with common scriptural and ecclesiastical emphases. A person can go from a Disciples of Christ church to the Methodist house of worship across town and know that it is the season of Lent and what that means.

Finally, the use of the lectionary may push the preacher out of her canonical comfort zone. Left to our own devices, most of us gravitate to sections of the canon where we feel most comfortable. For example, a preacher who feels at home with the Gospels may give the congregation a steady diet of Luke, but in the process fail to acquaint listeners with other parts of the biblical panorama. Biblical books such as Exodus, Esther, and Ecclesiastes are considered as inspired as the Gospels but frequently gather cobwebs in people's Bibles from lack of use.

Series

Another plan that some preachers use is a series of sermons beginning either with the needs of the church or with people in the church, or beginning with biblical texts such as the Ten Commandments or the "I am" statements of Jesus in the Gospel of John.

Eugene Lowry, Professor of Preaching Emeritus at St. Paul School of Theology in Kansas City, Missouri, gained recognition in two approaches to formulating a series: the "itch" and the "scratch." The "itch" is the need of the listeners. Begin with the itch, such as the challenge to the congregation to be more intentionally missional. Then the minister needs to find biblical texts ("scratch") that respond to the needs. On the other hand, if I begin with the texts, I need to consider their relevance to the listeners' lives. Lowry wants whatever sermons are preached to have both substance and relevance.

Two considerations are important to the preacher who does a series of sermons. First, each sermon needs to stand on its own. The day has passed when most members of a church will attend each Sunday. This means that a minister will leave many of her congregants in a fog if she begins her sermon, "As I was saying last Sunday . . ." or "As I've been saying to you for the last five Sundays . . . ." The preacher will probably be talking to herself.

A second thing a preacher should consider if he does a series is the number of sermons that will be involved and the time it will take to complete the series. This is not a concern with some series; it's hard to imagine nine sermons on the Ten Commandments. Which two are you going to fold into the same sermon?

Other series, particularly those that begin with the "itch" or the needs of people may be more open-ended. While there's no magical number, I usually operated with six to eight sermons in a series. The reason for this limited number is the "fatigue factor" both on the part of the preacher and the congregation. For example, a minister is usually energized and focused at the beginning of preaching a series. What happens, though, if you promise a year's worth of sermons, and you fall out of love with the topic by the sixth month? Perhaps, even worse, you look at the congregation after six months and can tell that the listeners have lost that loving feeling. It's much better to expand the series if the minister is still enthusiastic and the listeners seem to be responding well.

Book of the Bible

How will a minister focus on a particular book of the Bible? Or should she do it at all? A preacher runs the risk of the series being too long or choosing a biblical document in which he has an interest that, unfortunately, his listeners don't share.

With the negative said, there may be some value to prevailing through an entire book. Many of us grew up in churches where the minister leapfrogged every Sunday from one part of the biblical canon to another. While we were going from a pericope in Matthew one week, then to an epistle, and next a psalm, with lots of interesting stops, we had little chance in the sermons to engage and to be engaged by one book. We were bouncing all over the Good Book but never really landing and coming to Matthew, for example, in depth.

There are ways to avoid this. Suppose a minister who uses the lectionary decides one year that in the cycle of Year A, he will preach every Sunday from the Gospel of Matthew selection. Hopefully, by the end of that year, the congregation will have a much deeper understanding of the Gospel and will be able to understand it as a whole rather than piecemeal.

Episodic

This is not necessarily recommended, but it is often the way that preachers prepare sermons. Let's imagine the minister sitting in his office on Monday morning (probably a good time to begin preparing a new sermon). The preacher takes his Bible to try to find a text for next Sunday's message. He may have some vague idea of the need he wants to address, and he leafs through the Bible until he finds something that speaks to his topic.

This same routine is repeated the next week and every week. There's no planning ahead; there's no thought about how one sermon may build on another. Each week the minister is on the prowl for a biblical text.

The difficulties with this approach to sermon preparation are fairly apparent. First, it takes time that a minister may use in preparing the sermon simply to find a topic and a text. A minister is almost forced to make a quick decision about his sermon's direction so he can move on with the other steps of preparation.

Some ministers are reluctant to plan their sermons for fear either that circumstances may change and require a different sermon or that planning will take the spontaneous quality out of the sermon. These are legitimate concerns. Planning ahead is never the master when a situation arises that cries out for some word from God. In 2015, nine members, including the pastor, of the predominantly African-American Emanuel AME Church in Charleston, South Carolina, were slaughtered by gunfire as they gathered for Wednesday night Bible Study and Prayer Meeting. The accused was a twenty-one-year-old white man who confessed that he killed the nine people of color.

All kinds of issues are raised by this tragedy: racism, easy availability of guns, even the safety of people who come to the sanctuary of a church. This was surely on many people's minds as they worshiped the following Sunday. Even if she didn't base her entire sermon on this terrible event, a minister would miss an opportunity to say a redemptive or even prophetic word about what happened if she doggedly focused on what she had already prepared.

Sermon plans are designed to be flexible. Neither should they take any spontaneity from the sermon. Despite planning and preparation, effective preachers approach the moment of speaking the word with the sense that God is present and that we as ministers are ready to be used as vessels to pour the word.

These are just four ways to select a text. It may be that a preacher will use several different methods. For example, some ministers will follow the lectionary readings until what is called "Ordinary Time." Then they may preach a series of sermons that have particular relevance to their context.

Engaging the Biblical Text

Prayer

As the minister engages and is engaged by a biblical text, a spirit of prayerful openness to God should begin and permeate the entire process of preparation. This is not a self-centered prayer that God would "Make this sermon really powerful," and "Make me an acclaimed proclaimer." Rather, it is the recognition that preaching begins with the reception of the Holy One in our lives and that the ultimate purpose of our sermons is to bring our listeners as well as ourselves into closer relationship with God.

Our dependence on the leadership and presence of God does not excuse us from the work that we need to do to prepare a message. Instead, awareness of God as our guide and as the One we want to glorify helps us takes our offering to God more seriously.

Prayer that penetrates preparation makes us aware that being open to God demands that we stay open to doing our best to engage the text. Prayer is not a substitute for preparation. It's not a preacher's failure or laziness since God will supply the message. Instead, prayer calls us to give the best of ourselves since we are preaching in the name of a God who gives the best of God's self.

With our minds and hearts attentive to God in prayer, we can turn to the text. If it's a familiar text to us, we may assume that we already know it and do only a cursory reading. The problem is that such familiarity often deafens us to the sounds that we believe we already have heard. How do we read our text? If we know Hebrew or Greek, we read it from the original language. There are always nuances that are lost in any translation.

> Prayer calls us to give the best of ourselves since we are preaching in the name of a God who gives the best of God's self.

Then we read the text out loud because the Bible was originally a book to be heard.

Next, we read it slowly and silently, exercising the discipline of *Lectio Divina* that allows us to "chew" on the words. We pay particular attention to verbs and nouns. If the text is a story, we follow the movement of the narrative and the characters that move across the stage. We look for ourselves and others we know in the unraveling of the story. I may think that I would never be the self-centered son in the so-called Parable of the Prodigal Son (Luke 15:11-32), yet I have done life that way too many times.

Finally, we might have somebody else read the text to us. Maybe the person is not a proficient reader. But in the stumbling and mispronunciations, we can start paying attention in a new way.

After we read it, the text should become an integral part of our thinking. We think about it when driving to the hospital to visit a sick parishioner. We go to bed and awake with the words of the text bumping around in our minds. The sermon often takes form in those creative moments when the words of Scripture take hold of us and won't let us go.

Biblical Context

Most lectionary texts or biblical passages used in sermons are in the form of pericopes. And just as most of us prefer our doctors to use familiar terms, most ministers likely choose "Scripture reading," "text," or "passage" when we communicate this idea of "pericopes" to the people in our church.

Regardless of what she calls it, the minister needs to read that text carefully. However, each passage comes in the context of other events or sayings as well as in a document that we call a book. All of those books together make up the Bible.

As a minister is preaching from a pericope, it's important for her to know how that passage fits into the movement of what occurs before and after as well as bear in mind the major themes of the book in which it is found. It also helps to know the literary form of the document from which the passage comes.

If a preacher chooses a text from Jeremiah, he should know something about the prophetic genre and the overarching themes and development of Jeremiah. While all of that information won't be a part of the message, it will shed needed light on the pericope that is the focus of the sermon.

This is also true for a passage from one of the four Gospels. Despite some similarities, the Synoptic Gospels of Matthew, Mark, and Luke have different emphases. John's Gospel is cut from an altogether different cloth.

Recording Ideas

As the minister reads the text and the background material, he should keep track of anything that comes to his mind from the passage. Some may use a computer while others may write on notepads.

At this time, the purpose is not to get the point for the sermon but to brainstorm over the biblical text and record anything that comes to mind. What does the passage tell us about God? What do we learn about ourselves? Are there words that stand out? What is the movement of the text? Is there anything that happens or is said that seems strange?

We put the magnifying glass of our attention over the pericope and look at it in bold print. Out of what we record may come the point of our message, but we don't want to rush in a way that hinders our creative juices. Once we decide what we want to say in the sermon, then we have to say "no" or "later" to other things that we have recorded. The danger with many sermons is not that nothing is said but that too much is said, and the primary point gets lost in the wilderness of a lot of words about too many things.

> The danger with many sermons is not that nothing gets said but that too much is said, and the primary point gets lost in the wilderness of a lot of words about too many things.

Point, Purpose, and Plan

In his outstanding book on preaching, *The Witness of Preaching*, Tom Long speaks about the focus, function, and form of a message. While the words have changed, I, along with many others, am indebted to Long for the organic and organized way he has taught us to approach a sermon.

The *point* of a message comes when the minister knows clearly what she wants to say. In a simple, positive sentence that doesn't include "whereas" and "therefore," the preacher writes what she wants to communicate in the sermon. This part may be spoken directly or inferred indirectly in the sermon, or it may be a refrain that is repeated in the message, but the main function is to keep the sermon targeted on the one primary thing the minister wants to say.

What about the traditional three-point sermon? There may be times when a preacher wants to look at the main point from three different angles, but the last thing he needs is three separate sermons in one message where each of the parts is fighting for air time.

The *purpose* of a sermon is what the preacher hopes will happen in the lives of the listeners. Is he preaching a sermon intended to comfort? Is this a more prophetic message that challenges the congregation? Does the preacher simply feel the need to teach, to give people the information that they need involving a decision that looms before the congregation?

There are other purposes for sermons, but when the minister knows what effect he wants his words to have, the sermon is more focused. For those of us in the tradition of giving invitations or asking for responses, it keeps us from giving the congregation so many options that they become confused and uncertain about the choices they have.

Knowing our purpose also keeps the preacher from trying to evoke too many responses from parishioners during the sermon itself. For example, what if the first part of the sermon is designed to comfort the congregation, but halfway through the message the minister shifts into challenging people about giving more money to the building program? Again, as in a message that has multiple points where none can be developed, a sermon with more than one purpose becomes too busy. The congregation is left wondering, "Is this about comfort, or was the pastor simply setting us up for a plea for more money?"

One caveat should be added to the purpose of a sermon: every sermon should teach something, but that usually is not the *primary* purpose. A minister who displays her knowledge of theology or the background of the text during each sermon runs the risk of becoming both irrelevant and pedantic. Listeners want to know if the message has connection to their lives.

Once a minister knows the point and purpose of the message, he is now ready to develop a *plan*. A plan is how the minister puts together the sermon in order to communicate the point and the purpose. A plan is a strategy to help the minister stay focused and to cause the him or her to think about the most effective way to communicate the focus or the point.

H. Grady Davis called this the design of the sermon.[1] More recently, Paul Scott Wilson urged ministers to ponder the poetry of the message.[2] In designing or planning a sermon, a minister needs to consider several things.

First, you have a number of options, and it's good to have several ways to create a sermon at your disposal. Second, don't try to imitate or feel intimidated by preachers who have developed their own styles. We can learn much from Fred Craddock's inductive style and ability to tell stories, but if we try to imitate Craddock, most of us are going to come off as something that we're not. Find some plans for sermons that fit your persona and gifts and go with those.

Third, in fashioning a sermon, don't neglect the flow of the biblical text. This is particularly true of narrative passages of Scripture. The writers in the Bible were good storytellers, so we don't want to neglect what we already have at our disposal.

Finally, ministers should not become so enamored of a unique sermon form that the plan for the sermon trumps the point they want to make. Those who preach want to avoid the form of the message being so tricky and cute in that listeners are left scratching their heads and thinking, "There must be a point in all of this, but for the life of me I have no idea what it is."

The plan of the message also includes any stories or illustrations that we use to make the point. Ultimately, though, preachers need to ask themselves after they have prepared the sermon, "Is this clear and convincing to me?" If it doesn't pass the preacher test, it won't pass the parishioner test. Let's move on to how we connect to our listeners.

Notes

1. Henry Grady Davis, *Design for Preaching* (Philadelphia: Fortress Press, 1958).

2. Paul Scott Wilson, *Preaching as Poetry: Beauty, Goodness and Truth in Every Sermon*, The Artistry of Preaching Series (Nashville: Abingdon Press, 2014). Wilson does not say that every sermon should be a poem. Rather, the construction and language of the sermon should reflect the evocative quality of a moving poem.

Chapter 5

Connecting with Our Listeners

Despite the best intentions and best practices of sermon delivery, there is simply no substitute for the connection of a genuine preacher/parishioner relationship. The primary setting for the preaching event is, after all, community worship including a body of believers and the resident pastor. Parishioners will gladly listen to the dry delivery of a pastor who has supported them through thick and thin over the seamless delivery of a seasoned homiletician who simply does not invest in relationships.

The basics of pastoral care fall outside the scope of this project, but suffice it to say that spiritual support and Christian discipleship build the frame on which pastor and parishioner grow together. This point cannot be overstated![1]

Such connections occur in many ways, both outside and inside the preaching event itself.

Connecting with Listeners Outside the Preaching Event

Connections with listeners may originate from a variety of sources, most of which include gallons of coffee consumed cup by cup and thousands of lunches. Successful approaches may include the following:

- Friendships that emerge simply because some people happen to click naturally
- Reactive pastoral care at times of crisis, surgery, unforeseen transitions, etc.
- Proactive pastoral care in anticipation of upcoming transitions and events like baptisms, weddings, high school graduation, various types of anniversaries, and caregiver roles for grandkids and elderly parents
- Leadership development through regular interactions with deacons, elders, administrative boards, and staff
- Praying through the roster/directory and birthday greetings
- Participating in the local economy with an openness of heart
- Prayer-walking the neighborhood with a discerning presence
- Small group conversations with various demographics
- Formal and informal settings for table fellowship
- Worship committee and other structures for feedback
- Reaching out to predecessors in the local pulpit and neighboring clergy from the community
- Recordings, digital media, and social media
- Communicating upcoming texts and topics with musicians and other leaders

I also strongly encourage ministers to help parishioners prepare for the preaching event by communicating the text and/or topic in advance of Sunday. Simple methods might include emailing the bulletin to the congregation on Friday or sharing information via social media.

Connecting with Listeners at the Time of the Preaching Event

In addition to pastoral care and other forms of building relationships between preacher and parishioner, connection occurs at the preaching event itself. Most successful ministers try to arrive to the worship space early and stay late, making as many verbal and nonverbal contacts as possible. In all but the largest churches, ministers may also employ an awareness of which parishioners have recently returned after an absence (emergencies, funeral, travel) and what events lie ahead that will pull congregants away (transitions, vacations, surgeries). A pat on the shoulder or a knowing nod of the head on the eve of an anniversary can open the door for an extra level of connection with a specific parishioner on a particular Sunday.

Some clergy give consideration to connecting with listeners when they decide where to sit and how to dress. Starting the service seated among the congregation may offer the subtle theological statement that the proclaimer comes forward as one voice from among the people. General awareness of attire may also foster connections or at least avoid off-putting awkwardness.

Since there are so many types of preaching events, there are also many different examples of connection (or lack thereof) once the preaching event is under way.

Preaching to the Unknown Listener

There are situations when we genuinely do not know our listeners.

Pulpit exchange. Two different homogeneous ethnic congregations who swap proclaimers for a Sunday may create a setting in which preacher and congregation feel equally disconnected from each other.

New and/or young minister. The classic source of hilarity and sorrow for youth pastors and other staff ministers is only getting to preach once a year, usually the Sunday after Christmas when half the church is away. How does one possibly deliver a succinct, coherent sermon to people he or she hasn't addressed publicly in a year?

New parish. I've stepped midstream into a rushing, 150-year-old river. I have little to no idea what lies beyond the bend downstream or submerged beneath the surface.

Guest preacher. Perhaps filling in for a friend or a vacationing colleague, I may have some understanding of what the (absent) host pastor would like me to say, but I know little of the other side of the story.

In such situations, ministers may find it helpful to select themes that are virtually universal to all people, regardless of setting. Examples would include the salvific work of Jesus, faith, hope, love, and peace. Interim ministers recognize another universal theme: anxiety associated with transition. Even without specialized training as an intentional interim (training I highly recommend!), a good preacher during the interim will recognize the opportunity for an inspirational sermon series from an especially relevant passage of Scripture, such as the first several chapters of the book of Acts.

Preaching that Does Not Connect with Listeners

We've all been there. The joke that seemed so humorous falls flat. The clever remark sounds crass. The invigorating research translates into boring data. The profound observation draws an audible yawn. Chuck and I have both experienced the nightmarish moment when a parishioner announces, "I'm leaving the church, and your preaching is the reason." Simply put, if a minister does much preaching of any sort on a regular basis, she will have an occasion when the connection simply is not there.

The reality is that it's rarely so bad. It would be a truly unusual situation for a parishioner to find preaching so distant or disconnected that he chose to leave the church. Nevertheless, some listeners genuinely struggle to identify with a particular preacher.

There are even strange circumstances of unique settings/roles that cause the preacher to feel the disconnect, even if listeners may not. For example, a wonderfully gifted speaker serving as a hospital chaplain once described the many problems he faced when scheduled to preach the chapel sermon in a large metro hospital. The chapel was completely empty at the appointed time—save for the video camera that would provide a live feed throughout the hospital via closed-circuit television. Was anyone watching? He struggled to clarify and control his emotions in such a challenging setting.

Never underestimate the wisdom of the familiar adage *"you may be planting a seed."* It may be that your message, which does not seem to connect in the moment, somehow establishes a foothold for the gospel within the life of a listener. Chuck opened this book with the metaphor of preaching as offering, which is perhaps the best reminder after a sermon that seems to connect with no one. One treasured mentor even developed the personal discipline of reading the classic John Claypool sermon "Who Is Your Audience?" every Sunday morning.[2]

Preaching that Connects in Spite of Everything I Do

Other times, I have trudged from my office to the sanctuary knowing with absolute certainty at every step that the sermon I was about to deliver was the worst collection of drivel ever assembled. A week later, the accolades continued to roll in as I picked up my jaw off the floor for the umpteenth time.

Never underestimate the mysterious role of the Holy Spirit. From an awareness of this reality, a minister may pray before every sermon, "God, please speak through me and in spite of me." I also find that last-minute adjustments to my sermon notes may allow me to connect with someone in a way I did not anticipate until seeing her face to face on Sunday morning. I am not advocating that ministers should knowingly put off until the last minute the finishing touches of their sermons. I am simply saying that we need to have some flexibility for the lives of our parishioners on a particular day.

Preaching that Connects with What Listeners Need yet Refuse to Hear

I recall former seminarians who proudly announced that they were "prophetic" preachers come to whip the church into shape. Of course, the purpose of prophetic preaching is not to beat up parishioners but rather to speak truth to power, often while in the presence of a congregation. The goal is not a verbal assault that creates barriers, perhaps taking months or years to erase. A better goal would be to build bridges to new faith possibilities.

From time to time, I have confused a congregant's refusal to hear me with refusal to deal with a text or topic. This may not necessarily be the case. Sometimes I address a topic in a way that makes it nearly inaccessible for the congregation.

Difficult topics are best introduced through solid biblical examples. This sounds straightforward, but I have witnessed preachers across the political spectrum who followed a party line on a particular issue and never dealt with the Scripture on a controversial topic. Many churchgoers will consider a new viewpoint as long as it is *clearly* grounded in the Bible. Be absolutely certain that you have explained your train of thought, with biblical examples, from Point A to Point B. It may also be helpful to spend time reflecting on or even visualizing a journey over many months and years with the same group of people. Self-talk might include the reminder to myself that there will be more time and other occasions when I can address this topic again and go further.

Preaching that Connects with What Listeners Want to Hear

There is no pejorative language implied here. Most established congregations have a shared or even inherited sense of tradition. In the twenty-first century, these preferences still matter a great deal, and complex church systems may have multiple groups with their own preferences, even if (hopefully) these groups have chosen to coexist peacefully. Newer congregations, even house churches, will soon develop a sense of self. Such identity usually includes a normative experience of preaching, including a type of sermon the parishioners want to hear.

It makes sense when I consider the corollary in my personal life. I have strong preferences in the literature I read and where I get my news. If I'm honest with myself, I make these choices largely because of how they make me feel. Certain journalists inspire me; certain television programs entertain me; others elicit emotional responses that drain my energy instead of lifting me up. Congregations may have similar, valid preferences for their preaching because they know what type of sermon experience motivates them to walk in the footsteps of Jesus. Of course, it may also be the case that parishioners like a certain type of preaching because it helps them ignore the teachings of Christ or justify unChristlike behavior, but it has been my experience that most worshipers are genuinely trying their best—most days—to grow as disciples.

Preaching ministers may find it difficult to introduce new approaches that differ from what listeners want to hear. I am not only referring to the common, though often challenging, transitions that naturally accompany the change from one pastor to the next. Rather, I would urge caution when a preaching minister wishes to introduce a major permanent change to the context in which worship happens. In the twenty-first century, two examples especially come to mind: use of the lectionary and digital media, respectively.

Lectionary. When arriving in a congregation, a wise minister will assess whether the prevailing style is embraced by the church or was merely the personal preference of a predecessor. To a congregation with roots in an evangelical ethos (as most Baptist churches in the southern United States are), the introduction of the lectionary can seem like a whole new world. Parishioners accustomed to a local pastor who selects specific texts with the local church in mind may have difficulty with the concept of a group of scholars from far-off places selecting a block of texts for several seasons, leaving the idea of the lectionary rather fuzzy and even off-putting. The lectionary may be more problematic than helpful when it is presented as a prescriptive as a guide for worship instead of as a tool for the suggestion of possible sermon texts. To the worshiper, the assortment of Psalms and other texts can seem random or disjointed, especially in an era when the definition of "regular" worship is moving toward once a month or twice a quarter. If a worshiper has not attended a service in quite a while, she may struggle to make a mental connection between the psalm from six weeks ago and the New Testament epistle for today. It may even be unnecessary to use the phrase, "The lectionary text for today."

In order to use the lectionary well, a minister might start with the High Holy Days of the church: Christmas and Easter. During these seasons, there is significant overlap between what parishioners expect (and need) to hear and the texts selected by the lectionary committee, albeit with a rotation of Scriptures that may expand the sermon experience slightly for both preacher and parishioner. In different years, use different Christmas and Easter texts. Continue expanding use of the lectionary by grouping the texts into units.

Over the course of a month or a season, give clear promotion and weekly explanation of a series of lectionary texts. For example, a minister might announce five weeks of the Sermon on the Mount, eight weeks of Psalms of Lament, or a journey through the letter to the Philippians.

Further caution and patience may serve a minister in selecting attire. The parishioner familiar with the priesthood of the believer may struggle to understand why a minister seems to prefer setting himself apart from the rest of the congregation by wearing a liturgical robe. Use of the lectionary (or not) does not dictate the clothing style of a local minister.

Digital Media. The introduction of digital media can feel as abrupt as the lectionary, or even more so. When done well, digital media can offer significant practical gains, such as making text and song lyrics large enough to be legible for people with failing eyesight. When done poorly, such technology can feel like unnecessary sensory overload.

There are horror stories of digital media used poorly. Especially when introducing a new piece of equipment or software, or when welcoming a new volunteer to this ministry, the tech crew may need a more sophisticated document than the bulletin in order to prepare properly. A "detailed order of service" can contain all of the behind-the-scenes information required to make digital media helpful instead of distracting. (I describe this document more in the conversation with Chuck in chapter 8.)

One guiding principle is for ministers to make any major transition with a commitment to quality over style. If we do things well—carefully, respectfully, and slowly—we may have a greater chance for the congregation to shift with us from what they want to hear to what we deeply believe they need to hear. Such patience and caution may be guiding principles for most successful transitions in established congregations. Equally important will be the practice of ample communication, which may even feel to the minister like over-communication. While navigating cultural change, communication is almost a good in itself. I experience this reality every year when it is time to promote missions offerings for our various ministry partners and long-time members of the church ask, "Now, could you tell me again the difference between these two organizations?"

Margaret Marcuson encourages ministers to consider the witness of the peach tree. For three long years after planting a peach tree, the farmer can expect no peaches. Be patient. Fruit bearing takes time. Drawing upon this and other examples, Marcuson wisely adopts this rule of life for ministers: everything takes eight times as long as it's supposed to.[3]

Preaching that Connects with What Listeners Need and Agree to Hear

The sweet spot for connecting with our listeners lies in preaching that connects with what listeners need *and* agree to hear. For example, in some settings, I may not be able to do much with a topical sermon on ecumenism or interfaith dialogue. But during the week that I started writing this chapter, there was a mass shooting of journalists in Paris. My people are willing to hear this Sunday what they need to hear about violence and faith.

The capacity for this type of shared experience grows with time and trust. Relationships through pastoral care and other connections make such progress possible. In my current setting, I have found that parishioners with varying definitions of religious liberty will give enthusiastic attention on Religious Liberty Sunday if it is scheduled for the Sunday closest to Independence Day. Even so, I do not attempt to recreate Religious Liberty Sunday every week.

Finally, we ministers need to give ourselves grace not to preach every week at the intersection of what listeners need and agree to hear. Parishioners have genuine needs other than to be challenged or even confronted on a weekly basis. There are also times when what parishioners both need and want to hear will be the old, old story of Jesus and his love. In fact, a general rule of thumb may serve ministers well: before leaving the study or coffee shop, write a one-sentence answer to this question: "Where is the good news that *feels* good to listeners in this sermon?"

Notes

1. Helpful texts on pastoral care abound. For a classic introduction to the philosophy of pastoral care, see Wayne Oates, *The Christian Pastor*. For a more concise presentation well suited for continuing education, see John Patton, *Pastoral Care: An Essential Guide*. For a practical introduction to the clinical aspects of the pastoral visitation experience, see William D. Justice, *Training Guide for Visiting the Sick*. For guidance in pastoral conversations that shape personal meaning in both crisis and everyday situations, see Suzanne Coyle, *Uncovering Spiritual Narratives: Using Story in Pastoral Care and Ministry*.

2. See John Claypool, *The Light Within You* (Waco TX: Word, 1983) 43–50.

3. Margaret J. Marcuson, *Leaders Who Last: Sustaining Yourself and Your Ministry* (New York: Seabury Books, 2009) 83, 143.

Chapter 6

Connecting with Our Delivery

Delivery matters! I would even say that delivery matters slightly more than content. These two walk hand in hand in order to maximize the potential of the preaching event. But what are the most effective practices for delivery? What is the best style for delivery?

I would like to suggest that many preaching ministers are fully capable of pushing beyond a favorite style, a most comfortable method of delivery. For example, the congregation I serve is the "church next door" to Georgetown College in Kentucky. Each spring, we host annual revival services that honor the legacy of Bishop College in Dallas, Texas. Prominent ministerial alumni from Bishop make what has become a pilgrimage to central Kentucky. Despite smaller numbers than any of these ministers encounter on a typical Sunday in their respective parishes, they preach inspired sermons with visible emotions. Each year, there is a tender moment when one of the proclaimers looks out into the congregation and recognizes an old friend, colleague, or classmate he hadn't seen in ages.

The annual Bishop Revival exposes the limitations that individual ministers sometimes put on their own style. To be sure, I do not preach like Ralph West or Kenneth Spears—yet there is a deepening connection that happens throughout the revival week and from year to year. The deacons of my church find themselves enriched after sitting with a new style for a revival week. Students in the Bishop Scholar tradition who have worshiped in a predominantly Anglo congregation for a week find themselves drawn into Christian hospitality. Even the notable African-American preachers who headline the Bishop event remark on the surprising feelings of coming home that they associate with the event. In short, virtually every participant transcends the limitations of style and delivery to the greater collective good and the undeniable glory of God.

In contrast with such an affirming setting, I found myself surprised and disappointed by the conversation in the Baptist blogosphere and news circles that followed the recent death of Fred Craddock. Was it really necessary to degrade him posthumously? Was it really appropriate to publish such content, even if to oppose it? Could not practitioners of differing methods have chosen simply to celebrate that good preaching comes in all shapes, sizes, and methodologies? Does it not go without saying that ineffective preaching is all around us, too?

Every delivery style has its limitations. Every one. Without exception. For example, what passes for narrative preaching can sound like anemic stories and dry storytelling. Likewise, the expository sermon can come across as little more than a tour of the concordance with no honest biblical literacy on any individual passage. Every delivery style has its limitations. Every one. Without exception.

In many mainline and mainline-esque settings, a current trend has emerged. Carefully manuscripted sermons are read word for word in the pulpit. Like every other, this delivery style has its strengths and limitations. On the one hand, the approach is excellent for blogging and interactions over social media. It is ideal for a written response to a passage or idea from a published author. It is suited perfectly for those moments, whether formal or especially sensitive, when I need to be certain to have selected every word with careful precision. On the other hand, one of its limitations is that in the experience of the listener, manuscripts read from the pulpit are often incredibly, sometimes impossibly difficult to follow. This limitation can become especially pronounced when the speaker moves from one block quotation to another, no matter how renowned the original authors may be.

The history of this approach probably originates in seminaries and divinity schools where a central form of communication remains, by necessity, the research or exegesis paper. One can hardly imagine theological education without these assignments in theology and biblical studies courses, because they suit these disciplines so well. In preaching classes, however, the research paper gets a twist in the form of a written manuscript so a professor has something tangible on which to provide written feedback and a grade. As students move through the semester, a syllabus may require them to share manuscripts with each other or even preach sermons in front of each other. As a result, a conversation ensues consisting of beautifully crafted manuscripts that echo the content of classroom seminars, endowed lecture series, and essays from assigned reading. This is wonderfully rich within its context.

The problem lies in the fact that the church and the dominant culture are definitively not the same context as the academy! The church is not the same thing as an academic faith community, even in quite erudite settings. Laypeople usually have not attended the lecture series and did not sit in for the preaching class. They lack the shared experiences and glossary of terms that emerge within the classroom.

More importantly, and more universally, the human brain handles language differently depending on whether it is written or oral. In other words, while reading a text, the eye can process a highly complex sentence. While listening to spoken words, however, the brain must rely on subject and verb fairly early in the sentence in order to keep up. Complex written sentences beginning with three dependent clauses on the front end, while delightful to read on the printed page, make for a maddening auditory experience.

Conscientious preachers have several options for dealing with these concerns. One may choose to maintain complex sentence structures of written communication in the sermon, yet speak slowly and deliberately. Another might give the congregation a copy of the manuscript so interested persons may follow along. I know one excellent pastor who makes a few copies for attendees with impaired hearing, which he then leaves each Sunday in a mailbox outside his office near the main entrance of the church. Other preachers keep the manuscript intact but rehearse delivering it passionately, often with positive results.

Some preachers have developed the ability to preach quite effectively from a manuscript. Few listeners who have observed David Platt following a manuscript to address the idolatry of southern college football or witnessed Bill Leonard using a manuscript to dismantle legalistic affronts to religious liberty can imagine more effective speech. Unfortunately, many week-to-week preachers give little consideration to how to deliver the sermon effectively while relying on a manuscript.

A common response to the limitations of manuscript delivery is memorization. In my personal experience, on occasions when I tried to deliver a memorized text, I ended up sounding robotic, completely lacking in eye contact as I attempted to recall the lengthy passage crammed into my short term memory. Chuck has rightly differentiated between a memorized text and one that the preacher has "internalized." The former often remains little more than a collected stream of words, whereas the latter comes across as more of a unified essence of the whole.

More practical than memorization, and frankly what I would suggest, is a method of delivery that embraces the sermon event as fundamentally a spoken/heard oral experience. The following are some elements of this method.

Consideration of Structure

I often begin a sermon with a familiar structure that allows me to focus on connecting with the congregation without relying on notes for the first several moments of my message. In this method I begin by . . .

- summarizing the series or season in the Christian calendar,
- introducing the topic or text for today within the larger series or season,
- reading the Scripture text or referencing it if it has already been read aloud, and
- describing the context of the particular Scripture passage within the larger setting of a particular book of the Bible.

After moving through these four steps, I look at my notes for the first time. Because the structure itself is familiar, I am able to keep my thoughts moving forward fairly clearly without interacting with the text too frequently.

Moments of Personalization

A preacher might follow Craddock and sermonize her own experience. During an otherwise scripted delivery, she might look up from her notes and describe a personal experience from memory, perhaps relying on one carefully worded sentence in her notes to tie back to the body of the manuscript.

Sections of Extemporaneous Feel

In research or casual reading, ministers may run across stories they wish to work into upcoming sermons. Practice telling the story like you would over lunch. In fact, work the story into conversation over lunch and listen to yourself. You tell it better without notes. When it comes time to preach, include a clear prompt in your notes and retell your now-familiar lunchtime story.

Rehearsal

I've learned this lesson the hard way. After a truly terrible experience in college where I attempted to deliver unrehearsed a badly unfinished sermon, I vowed never again to attempt to preach without first doing a dress rehearsal word for word out loud. For several years, this practice also meant I rehearsed in the room where I would actually deliver the sermon. For the first several months in my current setting, I locked myself in the worship center Thursday or Friday afternoon and rehearsed until I was familiar with the upcoming Sunday's sermon. At the same time, I was acclimating to the room. This became less important after several months in my current church. I find it helpful to view this practice as if I were an artist; a musician would not play the organ offertory without rehearsing, and nor should I preach without practice.

Steps in Learning to Get Out of the Manuscript

1. *Include a beloved family or personal story in a sermon.* These types of stories are easier to recite from memory with only one or two phrases written down.

2. *Make use of asides.* Chase a brief tangent concerning an interesting bit of information uncovered in research that might be fully developed in a later sermon. It may not be exactly germane to the larger topic at hand, but it is not completely unrelated. In

the telling of it, the pastor develops the ability to look up from a manuscript even for non-personal content.

3. *Go through multi-step revision.* Start with a full manuscript and rehearse it as normal. After you become a bit more comfortable with it, revise the manuscript by replacing longer blocks of text with a few key words and phrases. Rehearse again, this time using notes instead of the full manuscript in some areas. Continue this pattern of rehearsing and shortening notes until you can preach it from just one page of notes, including certain sections where your only note is a single word or phrase. For short-term or one-time preachers, you might be able to go through this entire process in the preparation of a single sermon. For regular preachers, it may be more helpful to think of this as a *season* of transition or growth, one in which you attempt to move more and more out of your notes. In time, this approach will begin to shape the way you research and write the first draft, so it becomes more about writing for delivery from the beginning and less about revising for delivery at the end.

4. *Choose an event where a shorter homily is appropriate and go without a manuscript for the entire event.* This might be seen as a dress rehearsal for a typical Sunday. Use this time to focus on making eye contact with worshipers, at least one in each section or area of the worship center, or as many as is practical.

5. *Consider special occasions.* At times when the pastor would normally rehearse more than usual, such as Christmas Eve and Easter, he or she should try to enter the pulpit with the structure, content, stories, and delivery all but memorized. Carry just a few notes with you, and speak what has been practiced time and again until it becomes an overflow of the holy moment.

6. *On a more regular basis, including typical Sundays, deliver sermons in ordinary time without relying heavily on a manuscript.*

7. *Consider moving away from week-to-week preparation of sermons.* As I mentioned in chapter 2, I have found periodic retreat settings to be especially helpful. Use of the lectionary may also help a

minister develop this practice of planning sermons weeks or even months in advance.

In summary, I suggest that preachers may find a deeper connection with their delivery if they focus on the crafting of a brief document that will prompt them during the sharing of a spoken-and-heard message during a worship service. In other words, write less, edit more. Research earlier, revise more. And quote less, rehearse more.

Chapter 7

Is There a Future for Preaching?

Is there a future for preaching? In some ways, this is an uncomfortable question for those of us who have dedicated ourselves to the ministry of the proclamation of the gospel. My commitment to preaching makes me want to respond to the future of preaching by saying, "Of course, preaching will always have a prominent place in the worship of the church."

But maybe we shouldn't presume that the proclamation of the word will always be critical to the worship experience. Perhaps another way to ask the question is this: How is preaching

How is preaching changing, particularly with the influence of the mega-church movement and the impact of new, creative ways of communicating?

changing, particularly with the influence of the mega-church movement and the impact of new, creative ways of communicating?

Preaching as a Verbal Experience

Throughout my ministry, I have viewed preaching as an oral and aural event. As a proclaimer, my task was to pray through and study the biblical texts. Next, I would decide the point and purpose of the message. I would then try to shape a plan that considered how best to communicate the message. As a minister, I did all the talking, but with the hope that it would plant a thought or an emotion that would cause the listeners to continue the sermon in their minds and hearts.

Once in a while, somebody who heard the sermon I preached would question something I said, add a new insight, or ask me to clarify something. I'll always remember John Claypool's saying, "The sermon is the first word in a conversation." Of course, John had the marvelous ability to be thoughtful and provocative every time I heard him preach.

I wanted the sermon that I preached to be the first word in a conversation, but I was seldom privy to feedback. In hindsight, I wish I had constructed more opportunities to get better feedback.

Nevertheless, preaching for me (as for many of us) was my speaking and the congregation's listening (hopefully). Augustine's rules of rhetoric guided much of my preaching. Augustine said that sacred rhetoric should appeal to the mind, the heart, and the will. In other words, an effective sermon should teach, move the emotive sides of people, and prompt them to take action.

I would be presumptuous if I imagined that Augustine would approve of all my sermons. Many of my sermons were pastoral care messages. While these messages were usually well received by the congregation (because most of us are hurting in some way), I now recognize the imbalance. There were times when I should have been more courageous in tackling difficult social issues. Certainly,

I wish that I had preached more sermons that called the church to be missional and to make a greater impact in the world.

Despite my shortcomings, I still have a deep commitment to preaching as a verbal experience. Words can uplift, inspire, and call people to engage the world. While I want to be open to such things as using visuals, appealing to other senses, and expanding our technology, my fear is that, when used inappropriately, these things can be distracting and cause a congregation to lose focus on our message.

Preaching in New Ways

One of the most fascinating parts of putting together this section was sharing with Alan Redditt about new forms that are being employed in proclamation.

With the increase in technology tools, more ministers are turning to such advances when preaching messages and sharing sermons in digital form. With greater numbers of younger ministers who are skilled in technology, this method will undoubtedly increase. Many new ideas are taking root, so I will limit the discussion to several that I have observed and that Alan and I have discussed.

Use of Visuals

Again, the preaching to which I was exposed was an oral/aural event. Now, some ministers appeal to the sense of sight by using screens to illustrate sermon points, bringing items to the pulpit to elucidate something they have said, or using movie clips to underscore a point. There are numerous other examples, but the purpose is for people not only to hear something but also to see something.

The strength of this approach to sight is the recognition that we live in a visual age. Preaching developed before the advent of television and computers. Therefore, the fundamental way to communicate in church was through the preacher's speaking and the congregation's listening.

What concerns should ministers keep in mind as they appeal to more than the sense of hearing? First, some people in the congregation are so accustomed to hearing the sermon that introducing a visual aid is disconcerting and even disorienting to them. This may be a generational issue. Millennials and Generation Xers have grown up watching information as well as hearing it. Some of us who are older remember as young children huddling around the radio on Monday nights, listening to the "Lone Ranger" and having to create the action in our imaginations.

Regardless of our preaching method, we should never discourage the imagination and mental participation of our listeners. This is why I resist printed outlines of the sermon in the bulletin or fill-in-the-blank worksheets where we, for example, write "grace" when the preacher says the appropriate sentence. Giving people the outline of the sermon keeps the congregation from taking the sermonic journey and, in a real sense, creating the sermon for themselves. Filling in the blanks can make people think that because they know the word, they understand the concept. "Grace" is a wonderful word, but it is even more

> Filling in the blanks can make people think that because they know the word, they understand the concept. "Grace" is a wonderful word, but it is even more wonderful when the minister is helping us to internalize it and live out of God's unconditional love.

wonderful when the minister is helping us to internalize it and live out of God's unconditional love.

Satellite Churches

This phenomenon is especially popular among what we call "mega-churches." Usually, the pastor of a mega-church is an effective communicator. The preaching is often a part of an exciting and entertaining worship service that makes strong use of technology and other creative devices. Regardless of whether we agree with the theology of the worship format of mega-churches, the fact is that they are growing, and they are making an impact.

One way that these churches extend their outreach is through satellite campuses. When the original campus of the church reaches the saturation point, satellite locations are established in nearby towns. On Sunday, the service is video-streamed to each location. Usually, each satellite location has its own pastor whose responsibility is to care for the pastoral needs of the people at that site.

What attracts large numbers of people to these mega-churches and their satellites? It may be the preaching. It may be the quality of the worship experience. Most large churches have the financial and personnel resources to plan and pay for upbeat music, quality skits, and other components of the service. A word of caution: sometimes smaller churches attempt to imitate mega-churches, but they don't have the resources to do so effectively.

Maybe one of the attractive things about a mega-church is what psychologists term the "bandwagon effect." Go to almost any city, and you will find that the mega-church is the "it" church, the one that people talk about the most and that appears to be where most people go—the place to be!

The challenge of both the mega-church and its satellites is that they are often places where people go to *receive* but not necessarily to *give* of themselves. These churches work at involving people through small groups and a plethora of activities, but it's easy to remain anonymous and uninvolved when there are thousands of people attending the services.

The rise of satellite churches raises an additional question: Is it necessary for the preacher to know his or her congregation in order to preach effectively? People in satellite churches will see a visual image of their preacher, but he won't see them, and they really won't see him personally in the worship service.

Preachers in this setting must rely on their awareness of shared human needs, but they won't know if Sally and John have a child who is addicted to heroin, that Mabel is weary and discouraged from caring for her aging parents, that Harrison is questioning his belief in God, or that Lisa and Joe's marriage is falling apart. The distance between preacher and parishioner will grow, and the question is, "Can you be a really effective preacher without knowing your listeners?" That is a far different question from, "Can you be an entertaining and effective speaker?"

House Churches

While the prevalence of mega-churches is growing, we are also witnessing a resurgence of smaller groups of people gathering for worship and fellowship. This is not a new phenomenon. The New Testament indicates that the early followers of Jesus gathered in homes.

Why is there a new emphasis on small groups meeting for Bible study, prayer, and worship? Undoubtedly, part of the motivation is a desire for intimacy and connection with other people. The technological revolution that was supposed to give us more time has wound up taking more of our time and making us more exposed and more available.

People are riveted to computer screens. Texting, e-mailing, and tweeting have replaced phone calls and even face-to-face contact. Nobody is suggesting that we do away with our computers and smart phones. In fact, most people wonder how they ever functioned before this brave new world of technology.

The downside is that we move into our own worlds, never going anywhere without our mobile phones or iPads, never wishing to be somewhere without quick access to our e-mail or Facebook posts. For some, life in the cyberworld is satisfying, but many people long for the presence of other human beings and to be able to share hopes and fears with people who care for them.

The technological revolution that was supposed to give us more time has wound up taking more of our time and making us more exposed and more available.

It's no wonder that the intimacy of a small group of people is making a comeback. In this setting, preaching is different. Often, there is no professional clergyperson to deliver a sermon. The leadership of the groups may rotate from person to person, and the emphasis is on dialogue among the members of the group. Sharing of needs is encouraged, and others offer words of encouragement and support.

Those of us who preach may not be in a house church, but we can learn valuable lessons from that experience. What about our preaching encourages people in the church to connect with each other? As preachers, are we willing to share our own vulnerabilities so the congregation senses that we live in the same world as they do? Is there anything in our preaching that indicates that we need the care of others, or do we perpetuate the myth that preachers really don't need friends?

The call to be authentic is not a call, as someone has said, for "preachers to cut their wrists in public and let the congregation watch them bleed." Ministers face some issues that should be dealt with through personal counseling or individual therapy. As with most human beings, ministers are subject to depression, anxiety, and marital and family difficulties, and it's not a mark of weakness for the pastor and his family to seek appropriate help. Instead, it is a sign of wisdom and courage.

One of the easy ways that preachers can encourage identification and further dialogue with their listeners is through the use of "we" language instead of "you" language in preaching. If the preacher is constantly referring to struggles and problems in terms of "you," the impression is that the preacher is not part of the shared human problem. We need to be part of the congregation even as we preach because the fact is that pastors are also broken, experience fear and joy, and are often in need of the word from God that is continuously redeeming us.

A Future for Preaching

The fact is that we are living in a post-Christian world. Gone are the days when people would fill the pews simply because the church doors were open. More and more folks, especially younger people, are identifying themselves as "none" when it comes to a religious affiliation.

Yet there seems to be a hunger for something "spiritual." Preaching may have to be more intentional about addressing the deep craving for meaning that we seem to share. At the same time, those who preach need to challenge the church to be leaven in the loaf of our world. We may no longer be able to judge the success of our preaching by how many people come to hear us. In the final analysis, what matters is our faithfulness to the proclamation of God's word to others and to ourselves. Perhaps that's what has really mattered all along.

Chapter 8

A Conversation

Authors' note: This conversation took place in Alan Redditt's office after the rest of the book was complete. The purpose was to explore a few areas we hadn't covered or that needed to be expanded. It also gave us the opportunity to ask one another a few last questions.

Chuck Bugg: Alan, I know at Georgetown Baptist you have two morning worship services. One is a "more traditional" worship service and one is a "more contemporary" service. What I would like to know from you is, particularly as a younger minister, what factors shape your approach to the more contemporary service?

Alan Redditt: Sure. Those . . . are terms that I inherited, and they to describe what we try to do. When we talk about "more traditional," it's . . . more the mid- to late twentieth century. When we talk about "more contemporary," it's an acknowledgment of our worship space, just the reality that we worship in a 125-year-old space. It looks 125 years old. We have a tower and cupola overhead and a ceiling painted with a cloud scene of the heavens opening above; we have 30-foot-tall stained glass windows.

It would feel off-putting for us to do smoke and lights and a shield around our drums for a blow-out contemporary service, so we try to do what is authentic for us and . . . what makes sense in our worship space. For example, we do a lot with acoustic sound, we do a lot with mandolin, even some dulcimer, we do a lot with layering keyboard sounds; there's a Clavinova in addition to a classic baby grand piano, so our sound at no point is over-the-top electronic. We use a drum set, but it's electronic drums so we can adjust the volume. There's a rotation of vocalists, so it's a shared sound that is driven by classic sounds of guitars and piano.

I don't come in rappelling from the rafters; I don't use any zip lines or anything like this, and there are no grand entrances. My attire is still pretty similar to our more traditional service; I just change out of my sport coat and am still in a dress shirt and a necktie. The presentation is conversational, so I move around the platform. I try to think of natural transitions in the text that I'm preaching, and so when I move from one place to another on the platform, I am visually signifying to the congregation that this is a transition. We do offer some visual tech support, so the Scripture is on a screen overhead. I offer some basic slides—some quotes, images—and probably once or twice a quarter we will have video clip. We have additional tech effects—not that we have flashing colors or anything like that—but we will bring the house lights up or down. We try to play up the natural light that comes through the stained glass and so on and so forth.

Overall, we try to make sure that what we do is authentic for our space and who we are as a 205-year-old church. We try to take that tradition seriously. Something I have said to our church a number of times is you don't tell a 205-year-old church who it is. It tells us who it is, and we try to craft our worship appropriately. Our sound in that more contemporary service is somewhat like what you would hear on Christian radio but also includes elements of stylized hymns, updated hymns. Something that would have a very electronic sound on the radio is going to have a more acoustic sound in our setting, so my preaching mirrors that approach.

CB: I really like what you're saying. A few times when I have done interims, they've had a contemporary service, and I recall beginning the sermon with the needs of the worshipers. Sometimes I would begin a more traditional service with the biblical text and work fairly quickly through that text. I usually begin the contemporary service feeling that they needed to be brought into the message very quickly, and so I begin with what I perceive to be a need.

AR: For contemporary services, I also create a detailed order of service that provides more information than what you would find in the bulletin. Nobody on our platform is following the bulletin for the order of service. We're using the detailed order of service because it's going to tell us what's coming up, it's going to give us more information at each point in the service, and it's going to include tech information. That's valuable time developing an important document, but it is time that is taken away from the crafting of the sermon. Now those two things are complementary to one another—the creating of the sermon and the detailed order of service. But in more traditional settings I would not have that going on. In most traditional settings that I've been a part of, I've been able to go off the bulletin and not have to have all that additional information. So that's something else that's different between the two.

CB: Let's talk next about the *authority* question.

AR: Sure. Chuck, one of the things you've written about is the preaching minister, the proclaimer, who claims his or her authority as a speaker. One of the questions that comes to mind is about authority in the United States, where it is sometimes confused for *authoritarianism*. Even mentioning authority for some people evokes the idea of an autocrat or somebody who is heavy handed in leadership, but of course we know that's not the only example of authority. So I'm wondering if you can talk about how a preacher, a pastor, a proclaimer expresses appropriate authority when parishioners might be skittish about authoritarianism.

CB: That's a good point, and I recognize when I mention the word "authority" that many people can confuse that with authoritarianism. I want to make a strong distinction between my idea of authority and the idea of authoritarianism.

One of the reasons I believe many people have a negative reaction to the word "authority" is because that wonderful homiletician Fred Craddock wrote a book titled *As One Without Authority*, in which he talks about authority. He suggests we are moving through a time in which not only the people of the pew but also ministers in the pulpit question the efficacy of preaching, whether preaching is going to be a part of worship services in the future, whether preaching still has a place. It's interesting that Fred Craddock wrote this book, yet he is one of the most authoritative voices in the field of homiletics that we have.

One of the things Craddock says in *As One Without Authority* is that he doesn't want ministers to come to the pulpit with an apologetic tone or with words, as he says, creeping out the sides of their mouths. To me that is a good image of what I mean by authority. That is, ministers are given this gift of twenty minutes or however long you take to preach. No matter the preaching tradition, you're given that time to speak to people, so you come to that event with the idea that what you're doing is important—the preparation is important, the release and delivery of that sermon is important.

It's not that I assume I'm the only person in the room who thinks theologically. It's not that I'm going to disrespect my listeners by screaming and yelling. It's not that I'm going to become authoritarian in terms of my tone or approach to preaching. But I'm going to recognize the gravity of that moment of proclamation, and I'm going to use words that hopefully have the power to change the lives of people. I don't want those words, as Craddock says, to be said in an apologetic way as if I'm taking up people's time. I don't want them to creep out the corners of my mouth. I want them to be *heard*. I believe as a preacher and a minister that what we say is important. It is an incredible gift that few people have in their vocations: to have people sit and listen to what we have to say. Therefore, we want to take it as an important time.

AR: That's fascinating, Chuck, and as I'm listening to you I'm remembering some conversations that I have had or that friends or colleagues have had about this same topic but from a different angle. Sometimes parishioners are more familiar with an authoritarian approach because it's part of their background and is what is comfortable to them. What advice would you give, or what have you done if you've ever been in this situation, in dealing with the parishioner who is familiar and comfortable with the authoritarian approach and is pressuring you to assert your authority in ways that are not familiar or comfortable to you as a minister? How do you go about that conversation with that parishioner? How do you go about negotiating what your expression of authority is going to be in relation to that pressure?

CB: That's a good question because I have served churches where some people are comfortable with what I would call a heavy-handed, authoritarian approach. In fact, they would much prefer that I simply get up and tell them what the Bible says and what they need to do and put a period at the end of the sentence with no question marks. The way I respond to that is by simply saying that I have developed a way of preaching and an approach to preaching with which I feel comfortable, and it is not an approach that involves my being heavy-handed and authoritative. I would even bring them back to the Sermon on the Mount in the Gospel of Matthew. When Jesus finished the Sermon on the Mount, the one comment that was made about it and about Jesus' teaching was *not* that he had good words to say but that he spoke as one with authority. Authority, in that context, means a message that has been internalized, a message that you are giving to people because it has become vitally important to you. I would simply say to people the same thing that I would say to people who disagree with other aspects of the way I minister: that this is where I feel comfortable, and this is where I feel that God can use whatever gifts I have in the best way.

AR: Not that anybody would ever disagree with Chuck Bugg.

CB: Yes, I wish, Alan, but that has not been the case across the years. I have experiences of people who have said "just tell us; don't raise any questions." I think it reminds us that people listen in different ways.

AR: Oh yes, well said.

CB: I know what a gifted preacher you are because I've had the opportunity to hear you, and I've heard many people comment about your preaching gifts. What two things have you learned from others that have influenced your approach to the preaching event?

AR: Well, of course I have benefited so much by being surrounded by incredible examples and mentors and friends. I think of the peer group here in Kentucky that you and I meet with monthly and just the people I have the privilege to sit with and learn from, but there are a few that really come to mind. I was in that class at McAfee School of Theology when John Claypool came back to

Atlanta. We just soaked in the fellowship with the master, and it was a healing gift for all of us at a personal and spiritual level in addition to learning the craft of preaching. But two personal relationships stand out.

One is my mentor and friend Steve Hadden. Steve was our pastor in my teenage years and then hired me out of seminary, and what I learned most from Steve is the importance of finding your own voice. Steve's delivery was to go to the platform with a file folder, and he would open that file folder and within it would be a number of articles or his own notes from his reading. He has a voracious appetite for reading. I would watch him pick up these scraps of paper with notes that he had written to himself or excerpts of texts he had clipped, and move through the sermon by picking those up and moving them to the other side of the folder and then moving to the next clipping. It allowed him to be very personable. That's one of the most important characteristics of Steve's personality. It allowed him to be informal. It allowed him to get up out of the folder and look at the people and speak directly to folks. One of the things he would do—for example, if someone had loaned him a book or suggested an article, he would locate that person in the congregation and mention them by name, sort of give a nod, give credit. I've never seen anyone do anything like that in the pulpit, the file folder approach. I certainly cannot emulate that style, but it instilled in me that need to find your own voice.

This is something Eugene Peterson has written about in his autobiography. His son hit him with the revelation that all pastors have but one sermon—and Peterson wanted to join a church where the pastor had found his one sermon. He's talking about his voice—not simply saying the same words week after week. But he's saying that each of us needs to find our own voice. Steve taught me that.

Then I had a wonderful supervisor during my chaplaincy years in the hospital in New Orleans. JoAnn Garma is an Episcopalian, a wonderful educator within chaplaincy. JoAnn stressed to me as I was working toward certification as a chaplain that we have to be patient with folks because even though I may know my own voice and I may know my own identity in Christ, when I come through that door—whether to a oncology patient in the local hospital who doesn't know who I am or through the door of the sanctuary—I need to be patient and gracious. I need to know that my appearance may be welcomed by some, but something about me may be a problem for others.

I think of a time when I walked into the grief room in the emergency department and a woman immediately told me to leave. This was a middle-aged African-American woman who had just lost her son, and even though I don't look anything like her son, her son was going into the ministry and had died that day in a car accident. The fact that a young minister walked through the door meant that she could not receive care from me, at least not at first. There were other ways I cared for the family that night, but I had to take seriously that my presence was creating distance for her, and I needed to be patient with that.

CB: That is a powerful story about your going in and reminding this woman of her son. I think it's a good reminder to all of us that we're not necessarily in control of our images. All kinds of different things are going through people's minds; therefore when somebody says something to us that we may not understand on the surface, it may reflect what is going on in their lives and we need to be attentive to that.

AR: Chuck, we've talked a number of times about biblical literacy in local churches, that it is no longer safe to assume that folks within a congregation know a story or do not know a story, that there may be a wide range of levels of biblical literacy. I've shared with you the story of a friend who came to me after a service for children where I had read a Bible story from a children's Bible and this person said tearfully, "I don't know these stories. I've been a churchgoer and a believer for a long time, but I do not know the Bible. How do I start learning the Bible?" Could you talk a little bit about assumptions that could be made about the general direction of biblical literacy and what implications there may be for the crafting of sermons?

CB: For me, Alan, biblical literacy or illiteracy became an existential issue when I was pastor at First Baptist, Augusta. I would go once a year to the old College of Preachers in Washington, DC. Part of the discipline for that week would be that you preached your sermon before a small group of ministers. In the particular group to which I was preaching one week, there was a minister from Vermont. I made some allusion in that sermon to Abraham and Isaac, and it was predicated on the fact that people would know who Abraham and Isaac were. When I finished the sermon (and she was very kind in her response), she said something that really stuck with me. She said, "If you preached this sermon in Vermont, many of the people to whom I preach every Sunday would have no idea what you're talking about with Abraham and Isaac." I went back to Augusta and thought to myself, "I wonder if I'm assuming the people in this congregation, even though we are in the South in the Bible Belt, understand these allusions that we make in Scripture."

So I began doing a couple things in response to the legitimate criticism that she had made of my sermon. First, I try to stay close to a biblical text when I preach so that I can make sure that I have enough time to give light to that text. I try to avoid hop-scotching across the Bible to refer to different passages without any kind of background. I shouldn't assume people have the background to understand those references.

The second thing is I try to watch my language. To me, it's much like the analogy of a medical doctor. If I go to see a medical doctor about something that's wrong with me, I certainly want him to know all the medical terms; I certainly want him to have been to and paid attention in medical school! But I also want him to talk to me in a way I can understand. I believe part of the minister's job is to take what we've learned and to bring it into the sanctuary where people have not had the background we've had. I should not assume, for example, that if I use the term "soteriology," people are going to understand that I am talking about salvation. So I try to adjust my language to where I think people's ears are.

AR: I agree with what you're saying, Chuck, and it reminds me of our earlier question about contemporary worship or modern worship, and so a couple of ways that we have tried to do some of what you're talking about is through visuals, things like a series of maps. Jericho as a place name or Nazareth or Capernaum, even Jerusalem—parishioners may have little functional knowledge of where these places are, so sometimes we put a map on the screen.

I think what's most valuable is to have series of maps—a world map where the Holy Land is highlighted and a second map that is a closer view of just the Holy Land with the particular location highlighted. In a similar fashion, I will sometimes make a brief historical comment if I'm reading a passage from the Hebrew Bible. For example, I will sometimes say this took place at such and such time, which was about 800 years before Jesus. I don't give a historical lecture. They can go down the street to Georgetown College, University of Kentucky, if they want that much, or Baptist Seminary of Kentucky. I'm trying to instill in folks the cultural setting of Scripture, bridge the distance that removes us from geography and culture and language, and develop a sense of wonder about this ancient text that we are studying.

CB: I fully agree. One addendum is that there are churches where people have more of an understanding of theological words and theological ideas, so it may be in those certain settings that you could use words that would not work in another church. And, if you have people in the church who want to go deeper and want to understand some of these words and how some of these things fit together, oftentimes Wednesday night, in our tradition, would be a way that you could do that in a teaching setting where you can have feedback from people about whether this is understood, whether this makes sense, or whether this is heard. The problem on Sunday morning is that we have no set way for people to give us feedback other than a question at the door or something like that.

Now, Alan, as a younger minister, how do you work to identify with the concerns and needs of people in the church who are older?

AR: Well, it's a great question and certainly an area of ongoing growth. You know, we are in a church that has four or five generations represented. Folks like Reggie McNeal and others would say that the church has maybe never experienced this type of multilayered, intergenerational diversity, and so it is really challenging and something that is always evolving.

I would say the most obvious answer is through relationships, through pastoral care, and through formal and informal ways of investing in people's lives and allowing them to invest in mine and my family. We get to know one another, even if our pop culture frames of reference may be different. You know, I'm from the *Friends* generation, and that's very different from the *I Love Lucy* generation. Even so, there are areas of common concern—life, faith, family, loss, grief, sorrow—and we can identify these shared concerns and struggles. In pastoral care conversations where we are going deeper into those things, I can begin to identify some areas where people are asking for growth or where several people are experiencing the same issue. When I recognize, "Okay, in the last six weeks four different people have said 'I am really struggling with' or 'I would like to know about x, y and z,'" it helps me the next time I start sermon planning. I need to focus in *here*. *This* needs to be a sermon, *this* needs to be a series, it needs to be a point of recurring emphasis. It might play out in a number of ways, but in essence I'm just paying attention to what parishioners are giving me. These are the things that they are asking about.

One of the ways that I try to do this, try to connect with folks of different generations, is through some awareness of stories. So for example I had a sermon series on the Olympics back in the summer of 2012, and I was aware of different frames of reference. I personally could hear the "Chariots of Fire" story every week; I could watch the documentaries and all of those sorts of things. But we are so far removed now from Eric Liddell. That is a story that is only going to connect in a familiar way with certain demographics within our church, but for others it's a story they've never heard. They may or may not respond to it.

So I have enjoyed that series and in it I have given special interest to stories that are connected to a certain setting. People in our traditional service who know I am trying to pay attention to the different demographics in our church will hear me tell a story, and they may stay for the contemporary service just to see what I do differently to emphasize that same point in a different crowd. The average age, of course, is much younger in that contemporary service.

Another assumption I have had to overcome is the assumption about technology. Grandbabies have an amazing power to influence senior adults' and retirees' desire to learn technology, and so those grandparents are all over the computer for photos and videos that come in via email, Facebook, and now Instagram or other forms of social media. I can no longer make a clean distinction between those who are younger and know technology and those who are older and do not know technology. It is amazing to me that many of our seniors are so matter-of-fact in saying, "I Skyped with the grandkids over the weekend," or "I've got to get home from this meeting because I'm supposed to Skype with somebody back home." So I try to be aware of those types of changing elements. I know this is an area of concern for you as well, someone of another generation who is trying to connect with every generation just as I am, and I would be curious to know your approach to this, too. How do you as an older minister try to identify with the concerns and needs of younger church members and parishioners?

CB: One of the lessons I've learned painfully as a parent as my children were getting to the teenage years is that they wanted some distinction between me as their dad and their world. In other words, they weren't terribly interested that I was up on all of their culture as much as they wanted me to be authentic and real as a dad to them. So I carry that into the pulpit in preaching. I want to be genuine, authentic, and real. That means there are places I don't go in terms of culture because it's not familiar to me and not necessarily a part of my world. If I did go there, it would come off as sounding non-authentic. In other words, I doubt that the teenager listening to me believes that I am listening to her kind of music all day long. So if I pull in somebody from her world, it may sound as if I just want to say something that makes me identify with her. I'd rather do what I feel comfortable doing as authentic and real. I use humor a good bit, which is a good way of finding common ground with the people who are listening; humor can appeal to people of all generations. I don't use jokes very much in sermons. Instead, I try to find humor in the text. And so I find that to be at least some common ground, but I don't approach a sermon wondering how I can say something so that the sixteen-year-old girl in my congregation will think, "Now Chuck Bugg is really with it." More than likely, she will think, "He threw that in and he's not really comfortable with it. And it makes me uncomfortable for him to use it." So I have to watch that I am my age, and I can't be twenty-five when I come to the preaching event. I hope I'm not dull, but at the same time I don't try to work at creating interest by ticking off the groups that are well known to the young people.

AR: I agree that there are moments when it is clear that a connection is being made. Then there are other moments: I remember a time after services had just ended when I ran back in our worship space to grab my Bible, and close to where I had been seated I found a little piece of scrap paper where a note had been written during the sermon: "I'm not getting any of his pop culture references today." I thought, "Well, this did not connect today, so let's go back to the drawing board." I can err too much or lean too much on establishing shared ground on pop culture references, and that's sometimes not wise.

CB: Well, regarding your reference to the *I Love Lucy* generation, I think one of the things you want to do as an older minister is not rely on references that were part of your earlier life. As somebody once said it, "We continue to preach out of the time that we felt most alive in preaching." And so we keep going back and dipping into the well of something we did twenty-five years ago. What I don't want to do is live in the *I Love Lucy* world. At the same time, I don't want to create the impression that I'm immersed in the cultural stuff of this generation. I want to try to find common ground. And hopefully authenticity, humor, and some passion for what I'm saying become a shared passion. Don't feel bad about people's writing notes. I'm sure there were plenty of times that I just didn't find the note that people wrote: "I didn't understand a word of what he said today."

AR: Chuck, you've written some too about language. You mentioned earlier about language that is technical and may be inaccessible to people. One of the areas where this seems to happen in Baptist life is in the time that we refer to as an invitation or a time of response at the close of the sermon. In most Baptist churches, there is some sort of presentation and some sort of call for a response. You've talked a little about language that doesn't connect anymore. Maybe (and I stress the word *maybe*) it was the case fifty or sixty years ago that if I used the phrase "statement" or "letter" or something like that, it connected, but certainly today for most people that language is foreign. Could you talk about language that we might offer that would be an improvement? What are we trying to accomplish at that important transition moment in the service? How do we or don't we connect to the body of the sermon that has just been delivered or is still being delivered, depending on how you look at it? How do we handle the invitation today?

CB: Again, that is a good question, and I probably know more about what I *don't* like than what I've formulated about what I *do* like. I really believe it's important. Tom Long in *The Witness of Preaching* talks about a sermon that has a focus, a function, and a form. The "function" of the sermon, which I refer to as the "purpose" in this book, is *What do we want these words to do in the lives of the people who are listening?* We should understand not only what our focus is, what our point of the sermon is, but also what kinds of things we would like for these words to do in the lives of people. I think that informs the type of invitation we give because often one of the breakdowns I see in the invitation is that it is totally disconnected from the rest of the sermon. The sermon sort of ends, the minister slips into talking about four or five different ways in which people can respond, but the minister doesn't have enough time to explain these ways and the responses don't fit into the intention of the sermon. For example, if the function of the sermon was to comfort, then on that day when we give the invitation, we want to emphasize comfort. If the function that day was to challenge, then we want to focus on challenge.

I know that it's necessary for those of us in certain traditions to give the invitation following our sermon. Frankly, I wish sometimes that we had a little more distance between the sermon and the invitation because it puts pressure on the minister to try to give all the ways people can respond in the sermon. In my own invitations, I have left words behind like "statement and letter" because they're not very clear to people about what they're supposed to do. Are they supposed to bring a letter? Are they supposed to have a written statement of their faith that they bring before they come? I find myself wanting to talk in a more personal way about a relationship with who Jesus is and what Jesus wants us to be in our lives. And I even go back to what Jesus said to people, which is "I want you to come to follow me."

I would maybe try to say, "This is a time in the service where we ask you to come forward. What we're asking you to do is simply to take the first step to follow Jesus in your life. When all of us in this sanctuary took the first step, we didn't understand everything we were doing. We didn't understand everything about who Jesus was. But we took the first step in order to follow him. We want you to be a part of this church. We want you to feel that this is a place that will care for you, a place that can be a launching pad for you to care for others. So we invite you to be a part of the church. All you have to do is come to the front, and we'll do everything that needs to be done for you to be a part of this church."

I'm trying to get away from words that really don't mean much to people anymore. They may mean something to those of us who have been pastors and spoken them for so long, but a statement of faith or coming by letter . . . . I've had people say to me after a service, "Do I have to have a letter from someplace in order to come?" and the answer is no. A letter simply means we're going to write to the church where you're presently a member to tell them you're now a member at Georgetown Baptist.

Try to make it a more personal kind of invitation about what we're inviting people to do. We're not inviting them to make some abstract decision. We're inviting them to come follow Jesus and take the first step. We're inviting them to become a part of a group of people who are trying to follow Jesus and trying to make a difference for Jesus in the world. Also try to be as clear as possible, recognizing that it's impossible, really, to explain all of what this means in the invitation. About the best you could do is put it out there in a way that doesn't obscure the invitation for people, doesn't give them orders they don't understand.

Again, I believe I know more of what I *don't* want in the invitation. I'm still searching for ways to make the invitation more personal and to make it where people don't feel they have to make a prepared statement or have a letter that they bring.

AR: I agree, Chuck. Somebody else that I've heard talk about this is Marjorie Thompson, who spoke about it at Georgetown College a couple years ago. And she raised the issue of "pacing," or of rushing this moment. So many times, faithful churchgoer Joe Parishioner is actively participating, following along with the sermon, trying to understand it and apply it, when all of a sudden the sermon is over, we're into an invitation, and then through whatever piece of music is being used as part of the invitation and—done! And then a couple things are happening: one, it's over before they know it or before they get to make a response, or, two, the response that is coming for that person is lost in the rush of trying to get to the next thing, and, in some instances, ending the worship service itself and moving on to something else quickly after the heart of the sermon. Her suggestion is a discipline of silence, a moment of stillness for the congregation during which they can simply be still before the Lord. It might be a time of listening prayer, and it can be a time of journaling, whether that's a space in the bulletin or in the margin of their Bible or wherever they do that sort of thing. But a moment for them to write down or draw a picture of it or however they capture it: "This is what is going on in my life in this moment as a response to the sermon that I have just experienced."

I think there's some wisdom to what she's saying. I have certainly had that experience. The occasions are fewer and farther between now that I am sitting and listening to a sermon, but many times when I am in that situation I would like to have a little longer to sit with what I am hearing and experiencing before I'm asked to do anything with it. So I think pastors could shape the end of the sermon and the next moment in the service differently to allow for a response. It might not be the response of walking forward and speaking at the edge of the platform or, as some churches do now, walking to the back of the room to speak to somebody there. That may not change, at least not in any measurable way. But the spiritual response of the person who is sitting in the pew and is moved in some way might grow with some concern for pace.

CB: That is an excellent idea. Unfortunately, I didn't hear Marjorie Thompson when she said that, but I really like it. It reminds me that a book needs to be written on the invitation. I think most books that have been written about the invitation are very dated. The last book that I know was written by an evangelism professor at Southwestern Seminary by the name of Roy Fish. If there is anything more recent, I don't know about it. But we need a book that will give all kinds of suggestions as to how to do this.

And the second thing is to remember something that Tom Long says that is so important. He talks about the importance of connectors or transitions in the sermon, and where I hear sometimes the lack of real connection or the lack of really good transition is between the sermon and the invitation. We suddenly shift into a different mode of speaking. That's why I believe it is so important to honor the function or the purpose of the sermon and to let that lead us into the invitation. And to be the front end of the invitation that we give rather than by simply sort of stopping, you know, mid-sentence and then saying, "Now I want to invite you to come to be a part of the church. Bring your letter. By letter or by statement." We need something more that helps ministers who operate in the tradition of giving an invitation following the sermon. A lot of our friends in other traditions don't have to do that. They have other ways of getting people into the church or making decisions. But as Baptists, we operate largely in a tradition where people expect the invitation to come after the sermon.

Alan, I want to say it has been a good experience sharing this book with you. When I first approached you about it, I wanted the opportunity to see our approaches to things. For me, it has been a real learning experience to learn from you about things that are important.

AR: Well, you have been so kind to me through the years, and one of those kindnesses among many others was the invitation to study with you and to write. And I just continue to learn so much, but even more than that, to appreciate your friendship and mentorship. So I've certainly loved this experience as well.

CB: Thank you.

Sermons

What Matters Most
Scripture: Mark 4:35-41
Charles B. Bugg

Last year, my college alma mater, Stetson University, published its annual magazine on the subject, "The Meaning of Life." Students, professors, and administrators all submitted articles.

I was miffed. No graduates were asked to contribute, especially graduates who were ministers. After all—isn't that our calling? Aren't we supposed to tell both the suspecting and the unsuspecting what really matters in life?

I know not everybody cares. I've been in groups, identified myself as a minister, and the good times are sucked out of the room. Personally, I like to have fun, but the perception is that preachers are just focused on the serious things of life.

When I was younger, I boarded an airplane and sat next to a man. We said "hello," and that was all. After the flight attendants had served the beverages, and he had several of those bottles you pay $5 for, he was suddenly talkative.

"Guess where I've been?" he said.

"Where?"

"Atlantic City," he explained, "and if you ever go there, I want to tell you the best places to gamble." None of my church members would have given me that information, so I was taking it all in. Suddenly, he looked at me. "By the way, what do you do for a living?"

"I'm a Baptist minister." No more talk about casinos!

"My wife died several years ago," he said, "and I miss her so much." Suddenly, we were processing grief, and let the serious times roll!

This story in Mark 4 is serious, but like a lot of Bible stories, it has a touch of humor. Jesus has preached all day. As evening comes, he instructs his disciples to push the boat from which he's been preaching out into the water.

Jesus falls asleep. A whole day of proclamation can make anybody tired, and it says a lot that Jesus fell asleep before his listeners did. Asleep on a cushion, Jesus doesn't hear the sounds of a sudden storm threatening to sink the boat.

But the disciples are fully aware of the danger. Rushing to where Jesus is sleeping, the disciples awaken him and frantically ask, "Teacher, don't you care that we are perishing?" Jesus, now awake, calms the wind and the sea. Turning to his disciples, Jesus raises a life-sized question: "Why are you afraid? Have you still no faith?"

The writer Anne Lamott reminds us, "We don't always get what we want. We get what we get." The unexpected storm blows into any of our lives, and it's not what we wanted or expected. A child is critically ill. Our spouse dies. A marriage fractures. On we could go with all manners of storms. While the disciples in Mark's Gospel are not the brightest bulbs, I understand their fears. Don't you?

Yet in this moment where life is threatened, Jesus poses a question about what matters most. "Where is your faith?" This doesn't mean that the storms that batter the boat of our beings don't cause us to be afraid. No pastor worth her salt would say to a congregation, "You have a choice—fear or faith." Storms create fear.

"Where is your faith?" Perhaps what Jesus means is that in the unexpected twists and turns of our lives, we have to decide what finally matters most. Is it fear or is it faith? Or, more specifically, is it fear of the circumstances of our lives or is it faith in the Christ who is alive and awake to us?

Last year, all of us were deeply saddened by the shooting deaths of nine people at the Mother Emmanuel A.M.E. Church in Charleston, South Carolina. A group of African Americans gathered for Bible study and prayer welcomed a young white man into their midst. What they didn't know about this stranger was that he was racist. He listened to the pastor teach, but when the pastor asked the group to bow their heads for prayer, Dylan Roof pulled his gun and left a murderous carnage before he fled.

After he was apprehended a week later, he appeared by video to the family and friends of those he had killed. Listen to the way some of them responded to this person who had caused such a storm in their lives. "You killed my son," a mother softly said. "He had just graduated from college. He had such a bright future. But Jesus teaches me to forgive, so, as hurt as I am, I forgive you." A younger woman spoke: "You killed my mother. I loved her. She was the center of our family. But Jesus teaches me to forgive. So despite the pain I feel, I forgive you." And on and on went the expressions of forgiveness from the families.

How could they do this? These people had been hurt by an unexpected storm. Nobody would have blamed them for wishing the worst for Dylan Roof. Instead, they offered forgiveness. Why? Because they took seriously the call of Jesus to forgive. What matters most? For the families of Mother Emmanuel A.M.E. Church, what mattered was to forgive!

Jesus raises a life-sized question, but so do the disciples. Gathered together, they ask, "Who is this that even the winds and the waves obey him?" The disciples are rescued from the storm; now they ask themselves a question that matters most. Who is this? The wind and the waves obey him. The storm stops.

I wish I could tell everyone that if they follow Jesus, the storms always subside. I have lived too long and been a minister to too many people to make a promise that I can't keep. She was a relatively young woman when I was called to the oncology unit to see her. I sat by her bed as she spoke through tears. "I may never see my daughters graduate from high school. Who knows if I'll be at their weddings."

What do I say? It will be all right. Don't worry. Jesus will take care of you. A few months later she died. As I performed the funeral, I looked at her young daughters. Their mother was right. She will not be there when they graduate from school. She will not be there when the wedding march is played and her daughters say, "I do."

What do we say? Sometimes the storm is stilled, but often our faith stills us even when the storm rages. I wish I could stop every death, every divorce, every disappointment. But I can't. And in this broken world in which we live, Jesus doesn't choose to still all of our storms. In the midst of all of this, the question remains: "Who is this?" Or, put another way, "What matters most?"

When my daughter and her family lived in Boston, I asked if she would take me to see Trinity Episcopal Church. Made famous by the great preacher Phillips Brooks, the church stands in the middle of downtown Boston.

My wife Diane, our daughter Laura Beth, and I made the pilgrimage to Trinity. A gentle snow was falling. That night Diane found a picture of Trinity Church and bought it for me. The picture hangs in my office. Several people are making their way to the sanctuary for worship. Instead of a gentle snow, it looks like what New Englanders call a "Nor'easter." Driving snow and wind blow into the faces of those who make their way to worship.

In the foreground of the picture, a woman by herself, her umbrella turned inside out, walks through the snow and wind. Sometimes, I imagine what draws her to worship on such a dreadful day. Does she live alone and need the community of believers as her family? Is the worship service the one thing that gets her through her dreary week? I don't know the stories of why people come to a service when I preach.

Do you know what I pray? After the woman has sung the hymns, said the prayers, eaten the bread, heard the sermon, and the benediction has been pronounced, I pray that she will walk out the door and say to herself, "I know better what matters most."

Transcript and Preaching Notes for Sample Sermon
Alan Redditt

For Advent 2015, the Lectionary passages were from the Gospel of Luke. I decided to embark on a sermon series from Luke/Acts that would last several months. The sermon that follows is from Palm Sunday (March 20, 2016), picking up immediately after a pastoral greeting of guests. The text is Luke 19:29-46.

For context, it was also the day after the University of Kentucky men's basketball team lost in the NCAA national tournament—a huge deal in the Commonwealth!

For technical support of the sermon, a map showing Jericho, Bethany, Bethphage, and Jerusalem was displayed on a video screen.

In the interest of time, the sermon was shorter in our 9 a.m. more traditional service. It ended before the final story about Zezette and her friends. A video recording of this sermon is available at www.georgetownbaptist.org.

We continue today a sermon series from the Gospel of Luke and the book of Acts. On the last Sunday of November, we started reading our way through Luke's Gospel, beginning with the prophecies spoken over the life of Jesus. We saw his baptism and temptation, his early ministry in Galilee, his miracle working, preaching, teaching, and establishing relationships with others.

In chapter 9, we saw that mysterious and powerful moment when Luke tells us Jesus "set his face" for Jerusalem—he was resolved in his spirit that he would go to the holy city and all that awaited him there. We've seen that the shadow of the cross loomed over every step, every sermon, every moment since then. Last week, we saw Jesus arrive in the city of Jericho, his final stop before reaching Jerusalem, and meeting there a man named Zacchaeus.

Today, Jesus arrives in Jerusalem. Sometimes we call this passage the "triumphal entry" because of how Jesus arrives in the city, riding on the back of a colt, moving through the valley and up into the city, the people singing songs of Scripture, removing their outer garments and throwing them to the ground, taking down palm branches as they go. Sometimes we call it the "cleansing of the temple" because the first thing Jesus does when he reaches the city is to drive out people who have been using religion to make a profit on the backs of earnest worshipers.

But there's a moment in the middle that Luke captures so richly. It's found in verse 42. Jesus is riding on the back of the colt and comes up over the hill there near Bethany; he is able to see across the valley and look over into the city of David with the Temple Mount in the distance. And Luke remembers in his orderly account that Jesus was overwhelmed by the moment. In verse 42, Jesus weeps and says, "If you had only recognized on this day the things that make for peace!"

What brings you peace?

I can tell you what I *think* brings me peace. I can tell you, if I'm transparent, if I'm open, that I think I know what would bring me peace if I could only attain it or achieve it. There are many things that I *think* will bring me peace. I *think* a win in Des Moines yesterday sure would have helped. I think. I love the "mayhem" commercials; I can't even remember what it is they're selling, but

I think they're hilarious, the guy wreaking havoc on everything around him. I love the one that says something like, I'm a warm summer breeze. I have seven billion fans worldwide. But I'm just strong enough to blow through the kitchen window and lift the paper towel onto the hot stove and catch your whole house ablaze. I *think* a warm summer breeze would bring me peace.

I think I know what we as a people, as a society, sometimes think would bring us peace: things like financial stability. If only I could ever just reach that magic number, that threshold, if only I could ever have enough financial planning, enough savvy with the stocks, if only I could ever achieve my notion of financial stability, then I could be at peace.

If only I could ever just live a life without anxiety. How many people who are pursuing this goal are willing to self-medicate or are willing to enter into all sorts of destructive habits, relationships, and tendencies that are incredibly unhealthy in pursuit of the absence of anxiety, a target that is ever moving further?

I *think* we think, "If we could ever achieve 'enough,' whatever enough may be, if I could just gain enough, then I would be at peace."

We should know that there is turmoil in this setting where Jesus speaks of peace. This is not the absence of anxiety. We should pay attention to the context. Back in verse 27 last week, we entered Jericho and encountered Zacchaeus. There was a wonderful pronouncement; Zacchaeus had a breakthrough. We didn't get into it [in the message], but Jesus tells a story while he's sitting in Zacchaeus's house with the Jesus Movement, and the story closes with these words: "slaughter them in front of me." Those are the closing words of this fictional story that Jesus tells in Zacchaeus's home; the landowner in the story ends the story with that quote. According to Luke, Jesus then gets up from the table and pivots to the west and heads for the edge of town. No wonder he walks alone ahead of them out of the city and into the mountains, the Jesus

Movement trailing along behind him! Slaughter them in front of me? Jesus, you're supposed to be Jesus! That sort of emotional turmoil is still the setting as Jesus reaches these little communities of Bethany and Bethphage and starts to move toward Jerusalem.

We see the emotions of the story in verse 37 (the joy of the crowd), verse 39 (the frustration of the Pharisees), verse 41 (Jesus weeping), verse 45 (Jesus angry to the point of violence). And all the while, Jesus' face is set for this, for this moment, for this place and what will follow in the days to come.

I know what I think will bring peace, and I have some idea about what some of us think will bring peace.

We can also tell something about what the characters in the story seemed to think would bring peace. They thought miracles would bring peace. In verse 37, they are singing for all the miracles they have seen, for all the wonder-working, all the times they've been able to convince Jesus to give them what they want. They think these miracles will bring them peace.

They think emotional experiences will bring them peace. Well, some of them do; others think emotional experience will take them away from peace. The crowd is euphoric, but the Pharisees in verse 39 think it's all too much. "Make them stop, Jesus. Don't you hear the words they're using about you? Don't you see how excited the crowd is? Make them stop! They think emotional experience will bring them peace."

They think they'll be at peace if they witness the fulfillment of whatever particular version of prophetic expectation it is that they've bought into, whether it's from 2 Kings 9 where they learn to take off their cloaks and lay them down before the king, from Zechariah 9:9 where they're taught to place the coming king on the back of a colt that's never been ridden and accompany him into the city, or from Psalm 118 where they learn the lyrics to the song, "Blessed is the one who comes in the name of the Lord." They think fulfillment of prophecy will bring them peace.

But Jesus says they just don't get it. They do not witness the things that bring peace. None of these brings peace.

So let's talk today about what truly brings peace for those in Jerusalem in this Scripture passage and for we who live in the twenty-first century who, very much the same, desperately seek perfect peace. There are at least three places in this text that describe what truly brings peace.

First and foremost, what truly brings peace is Jesus himself, not the miracles or the teachings or the expectations fulfilled, not the lyrics to the song, not any of the trappings; these are peripheral, these are all tangential. What truly brings peace is Jesus himself. Coach John Wooden used to tell his players, "It isn't what you do, it's how you do it." That's why Jesus enters the city this way: instead of leading an army of warriors, it's peasants; instead of archers on the hill, it's children waving palm branches; instead of people adorned in splendor, it's people taking off their jackets and laying them down. Jesus enters the city humbly, even tearfully, because he knows what lies ahead. He's tried to explain it not once, not twice, but three times. "For the Son of Man must be betrayed, executed, and on the third day rise again."

It is Jesus himself who brings peace, the Son of God; as another Gospel would put it, he's "the Word made flesh," the very essence of holiness living among us. It is Jesus himself who brings peace, more than miracles, more than words, more even than scripture fulfilled, it is Jesus of Nazareth who we come to know more and more as the Messiah, the Christ, the Promised One, the Holy One, God's self.

Second, what truly brings peace is true worship. We witness it in at least three places in this text. The first is in verse 40. The Pharisees can't take it anymore: "No, no, it's too loud, and the words are all wrong! Jesus, make them stop!"

Jesus says, "I could make them stop, but then the very rocks would cry out." True worship happens when we join with creation itself in the praise of our God. When we recognize that the rock is our brother and the green grass . . . have you thought yet this year about just how blessed we are to be living in the changing of the seasons from winter to spring in central Kentucky? Thanks be to God! Somebody sing the Doxology; it would be appropriate! Right? It's not just the green grass, it's driving down US 25 toward Lexington and seeing everything that blooms currently in bloom; it's those crazy little hyacinths outside our kitchen window that waited one whole day after the final snow melted before peeking out in purple. The rocks will cry out because they know their creatureliness and they know the One who is the Creator. And so might we in our full creatureliness give praise to the One who has created it all.

The second place we see true worship is verse 44. Jesus laments, he weeps over the city, he cries out mourning over it, "You did not recognize the time of your visitation from God." Our God is still visiting. Our God is still present, our God is still active in our world and in our lives, and if we will recognize where God is at work, if we will seek to join God in God's work of drawing the world into a love relationship through Jesus Christ, then that too is an act of worship. Recognizing where Jesus is present, crediting God for the work that God is doing—this is true worship.

You know who normally gets the credit for such things in my little life? It's me. I almost always get the credit in my little life, but it is God who is making straight the pathways of righteousness in my life, it is God who is knocking on the door again and again in my life, who is opening doors for me to use the gifts and abilities— limited as they may be—for Christ.

The third place we see true worship is in verse 46, "My house shall be a house of prayer." Wherever I gather for Christian fellow- ship, whether the place has towering ceilings and fifty-foot stained glass windows or it's around the kitchen table to hear the word of God read—wherever I find the house of the Lord, it is to be a place of prayer. Not a place of opportunism, not a place of taking advantage, not a place of slander; it is to be a house of prayer, a place where the community of God gathers together in Christian fellowship in support of one another because we can do more together as sisters and brothers in Christ than we can do individually on our own. It's more than emotion that makes true worship; it's more than a question of whether my heart soars or if I just don't feel it today. True worship goes beyond the limitation of my mind or my emotion or my physical response to worship.

And what truly brings peace is also selfless sacrifice. All of the Gospels contain some version of the story of Jesus cleansing the temple. Each one records this story, and it appears in each one that Jesus is angry, he's frustrated, and it boils over and he turns away those who would turn a profit on the faithfulness of other worshipers. Yet there's more that is happening in Jesus' action, there's more than just Jesus being upset. What's happening here is Jesus pulling people out of the mindless habit of living for self. Not only is he aiding those worshipers who have come here after days and days of pilgrimage and wish to observe within the house of the Lord a season of prayer; he is also making it possible for those who are crooked businesspersons in the temple, those who are turning a profit on the backs of the faithful, to have an opportunity to become faithful themselves. He overturns and drives out, but even as the shopkeepers are chasing after chickens and scooping up coins as they run for the exits, Jesus is interceding in their lives. They may not even realize what Jesus is doing for them. He is pulling them out of mindless living for self. He is making it possible for them to return to the temple as a house of prayer. Pulling others out of mindless living for self is what we are all about if we are on mission with the Holy.

Throughout the next several days, if you read through the rest of the story, you'll see it isn't just those crooked businesspersons who will run and hide. You'll see first one and then another and then all of Jesus' followers, all of the Jesus Movement save for his mama and a few others, they'll all run, they'll all abandon, they'll all turn aside and deny that they ever knew him, deny that he ever changed their lives, deny that he ever showed them what true life was all about. And yet Jesus' face will still be set for Jerusalem. He will continue on, day after day, visiting the temple, confronting and overturning injustice, and inviting others to turn away from mindless living for self.

For example, there's a story that comes from Paris after World War 2 about five children who had lived together in bomb shelters during the war and often spoke of what life was like "before": before the war, before the bombs started falling, before they lived five years in a bomb shelter, before the rubble that was their neighborhood after the war, before everything changed. Some of you grew up in places like that where kids were all around and always together.

Now, after the war, they along with everyone else found themselves adjusting to the new sense of normal. One of them, a little girl named Zezette, was dying. Little Zezette was dying, not from an illness or anything diagnosable but from malnourishment because her diet was so bad. The rest of the group thought that if they could just get her a little more, somehow find her what you and I know as protein, she could regain her strength. Easter was approaching, and they decided Zezette should have some eggs for Easter, one a week for several weeks.

But they had nothing. Everybody they knew had nothing. Finally they hit upon an idea. One of the children, a little girl named Louise, could sew. The group decided she should knit something that could be bartered for eggs, because they heard there were people in a different place who had eggs.

Now these kids had been through the war. They knew impossible when they heard it. They went home dejected, each one trying to think of a way they could help. In the meantime, Zezette's brother Charles was put in charge of trying to lift her spirits, so he went home to sit with her and prayed over her day after day.

One day, Louise did not have school and so she stayed home to clean around the house. She reflected again on the fact that she had no materials to use for the knitting project. As she began to put more water in her washrag, her eyes fell upon that rag. Years before, it had been an old sweater that had belonged to her mother. It was far too filthy, too ratty to be of any use now. Nevertheless, Louise poured a bowl of clean water and placed the old sweater in the water to soak. When she returned some hours later, she emptied out the water, now black with grime, wrung out the cloth, and poured another bowl of clean water. She repeated this process a dozen times over several days until the water ran clear. Now, Louise didn't have any extra soap for the project, but the next time it was her turn for a bath, she skipped. Instead of using the soap for herself, she used it to scrub the cloth. Finally, she let it dry until it was clean, or as clean as it could be. Painstakingly, she began unraveling it thread by thread, tying the places where it broke, until she had several balls of yarn.

They didn't have any color. Nobody was going to barter for an ex-sweater that had been used as a cleaning rag for months. And so another little boy, Jules, went home that night and considered the problem. He didn't have any materials, but he did have time, so he traded his time in order to stand in line for the lady who ran consignment and needed some matches. And in this story I'm going to say that the dye she gave him was a bright royal blue, because I can do that with the story today, and I need it to be bright royal blue—or red, depending on where you're sitting today!

And so Jules dropped off the dye, and Louise went to work, and before long she had knitted a new sweater. Of course, she was limited by the still-ragged yarn, so the new garment had several thin, ratty patches that weren't much to look at. Little Paul spoke up when he remembered that his mother had long kept a bag of leftover pieces of yarn—nothing that could be used for any one project, but perfect to be sewn into the new sweater as decorative pieces covering the thin spots. When he approached his mother, he had to trade assurances that he would always and forever be sure to go to bed when his mother told him it was time and never to argue about bedtime again, if she would give him that bag of scraps. Sure enough, she did.

Now the group had a lovely sweater, truly something worthy of trading for Zezette's eggs. There was just one problem: there were no eggs to be found in the city. But Remi, the eldest of the gang at twelve years of age, had a bicycle . . . and courage. They decided that Remi would ride his bike out into the countryside in search of eggs. The next day he set out. He rode all through one day and into the twilight hours. As night fell, he realized he would need to find someplace to stay the night, so at the next farm where he saw a light on, he turned down the drive and pedaled up to the farmhouse, which was still bombed out from the war. A man answered the door and when he realized it was a child, he insisted that Remi stay the night. It was the Bonnet family.

Remi began to explain what had happened, and they began to weep. Oh, they were touched, but they were especially moved at the story of little five-year-old Zezette, for their little five-year-old Clothilde had not survived the war. The next morning, when Remi woke up, there were two dozen eggs laid out on the kitchen table next to the blue sweater. The Bonnets refused to take the blue sweater, saying it was far too precious to trade for eggs, but they instructed Remi to come back for more in two weeks' time. They also gave him directions to a farm further up the road that hadn't been bombed and might be willing to barter for the sweater. So two days later, Remi found himself struggling to pedal his bicycle back toward the city with two dozen eggs, five pounds of potatoes, apples, honey, butter, salad, and a chicken. And a promise that if he'd come back out in the country two weeks later, there'd be more eggs.

A few days later, the whole gang gathered for an Easter feast with all the food. Zezette managed to summon the strength to join them as they presented her with her Easter eggs, a balanced meal, and the promise of one egg a week for the foreseeable future. And one year later, at their now-annual Easter feast, after a steady diet of one egg a week in the rubble of the city after the war, Zezette was as healthy as the rest.[1]

Selfless sacrifice is as well the pathway to perfect peace. We find it in Jesus himself, not where I set him on a shelf but as he truly is; we find peace in true worship; and we find peace in selfless sacrifice. If that's the life that you know you desperately need to live, we want to give you an opportunity to choose it right now.

Sermon Notes

Georgetown Baptist Church, Sunday Sermon, Palm Sunday
March 20, 2016
Alan B. Redditt

Text: Luke 19:29-46

Series
Today
   - arriving in Jerusalem
      • triumphal entry
      • cleansing the temple
   - v42 Jesus looks across valley
      • v42 "If you had only recognized on this day the things that make for peace!"

What brings you peace?
- What **I** think: A win in Des Moines
    • "mayhem" commercial: warm summer breeze, 7 billion fans worldwide
- What **we** think: financial stability, a life without anxiety, enough

Turmoil in this story
-context: v27
    • Still in Jericho
    • Jesus "slaughter them in front of me"
    • No wonder he turns and walks ahead of them out of the city and into the mountains
-emotions
    • v37 joy of crowd
    • v39 frustration of Pharisees
    • v41 weeping of Jesus
    • v45 anger of Jesus
    • All the while, Jesus' face is set for this moment . . . and what follows

What **they** in the story thought:
- miracles (v37 singing for all the miracles they had seen)
- emotional experience (v39 Pharisees think it's too much)
- fulfillment of whatever version of prophetic expectation
    • taking off cloaks (2 Kings 9:13)
    • colt (Zechariah 9:9)
    • singing "Blessed is the one who comes in the name of the Lord" (Psalm 118:26)
- v42 Jesus says they don't get it
    • None of those things brings peace

What truly brings peace:

A. Jesus himself
  - John Wooden "It isn't what you do, it's how you do it."
  - the WAY Jesus enters the city
(more than miracles)

B. True worship
  - see it in 3 places
    • v40 "The rocks would cry out" (join with creation)
    • v44 "you did not recognize the time of your visitation
      from God" (recognize and give credit for God at work)
    • v46 "My house shall be a house of prayer" (prayer
      fellowship)
(more than emotions)

C. Selfless sacrifice
  - v45 Jesus cleansing the temple
(pulling others out of mindless living for self)

Story: Paris after WW2
  - 5 children (bomb shelters)
  - Zezette dying from malnourishment
    • Eggs for Easter
  - Idea: Louise should knit something that could be bartered
    for eggs
  - Impossible
  - Zezette's spirits
    • Brother Charles
    • Sat with her and prayed over her day after day
  - No materials
    • Louise
    • Cleaning rag = Old sweater
    • Unravel into yarn
  - Color

- • Jules
- • Dark blue dye
- Thin patches
  - • Paul
  - • Mother's bag of leftover yarn pieces
- No eggs in city
  - • Remi
  - • Bike into countryside
  - • Country home: Bonnet family
  - • Next morning: 2 dozen eggs
  - • Come back for more in 2 weeks
  - • Directions to farm that hadn't been bombed
  - • 5lbs potatoes, 1 chicken, apples, honey, butter, salad
- Easter feast
- 1 year anniversary:
  - • Zezette as healthy as the rest

Note

1. Paraphrased from Claire Huchet Bishop "A Dust Rag for Easter Eggs" in *Easter Stories: Classic Tales for the Holy Season*, Merriam Leblanc, ed., 285–300.

www.ingramcontent.com/pod-product-compliance
Lightning Source LLC
Chambersburg PA
CBHW052113090426
42741CB00009B/1788